WITHDRAWN

PORTRAITS OF THE BIG FOUR

of the Peace Conference

Count Aldrovandi   Sir Maurice Hankey   Professor Mantoux
Italian Secretary   British Secretary   French Secretary

SIGNOR ORLANDO   MR. LLOYD GEORGE   M. CLEMENCEAU   MR. WILSON

THE BIG FOUR

THE BIG FOUR

And Others of the Peace Conference

BY

ROBERT LANSING

BOSTON AND NEW YORK

HOUGHTON MIFFLIN COMPANY

The Riverside Press Cambridge

1921

CONTENTS

PORTRAITS OF THE BIG FOUR

IMPRESSIONS OF OTHERS

ILLUSTRATIONS

THE BIG FOUR
And Others of the Peace Conference

THE BIG FOUR
And Others of the Peace Conference

INTRODUCTION

It is by no means an easy task to analyze and compare the characteristics of the four statesmen who were the leading figures in the Peace Conference at Paris, or to state without reservation the part which each played in the negotiations, the motives which inspired his actions, and the success or failure of his efforts. It is therefore with a measure of hesitation that I attempt to judge the personalities of the Big Four and to give to each his proper place of prominence in the proceedings of that great assembly of the masters of political thought.

It is manifestly difficult to treat the subject impersonally and to avoid the petty influences which ought not to, but so often do, warp individual opinion and a just appraisement of public men. Yet it cannot be denied that traits of character are as frequently shown by trivial incidents as by those of greater moment, though

Introduction

it is on the latter that popular reputations are
founded. It is essential to a true estimate of a
man's character to give a right valuation to the
small as well as the great acts which go to make
up his life. With a lively appreciation of the
dangers of error, I enter upon the consideration
of the characters of the Big Four.

Until the President had been in Paris ten days,
after his return from the United States, in the
middle of March, 1919, the directing body of the
Peace Conference — or, more correctly, the Conference on the Preliminaries of Peace — was the
so-called Council of Ten, which, like the Supreme
War Council, was composed of the heads of states
and the secretaries and ministers of Foreign
Affairs of the United States, Great Britain,
France, and Italy, together with two Japanese
statesmen of ambassadorial rank. After that
time the Council of Ten was divided into two
councils — the Council of the Heads of States,
known also as the Council of Four, the Big Four,
and, by some, as The Olympians; and the Council
of Foreign Ministers, commonly called the Council of Five, or the Little Five — five, because
one of the Japanese ambassadors was included.
The latter Council was subordinate to, and sub-

Introduction

ject to the direction of, the Council of the Heads of States.

The Council of Ten consisted of Mr. Lloyd George and Mr. Balfour, M. Clemenceau and M. Pichon, Signor Orlando and Baron Sonnino, Baron Makino and Baron Matsui — or Viscount Chinda — and Mr. Wilson and myself. The Supreme War Council had the same membership, but had to do with the armistice and other matters of a military and naval character.

Prior to the President's departure for the United States on February 14, 1919, the Supreme War Council and the Council of Ten met thirty-five times. During the month that the President was absent there were eighteen meetings, M. Tardieu attending four of them in place of M. Clemenceau while the latter was recovering from the wound which he received from an anarchist's bullet. Lord Milner also had a seat in the Council, when Mr. Lloyd George was absent; and Mr. Henry White or Colonel Edward M. House sat as the second American member in the Council when the President was in the United States. After the President's return the Council of Ten met regularly seven times until, on March 24th, it was divided into two councils as I have stated.

[5]

Introduction

Between that date and the President's final departure on June 28th there were six meetings of the Council of Ten; and up to my departure on July 12th, ten other meetings. I was therefore present at seventy-six meetings of the Council of Ten or of the same body sitting as the Supreme War Council. This gave me opportunity to become acquainted with the four heads of states and to gain some clear impressions as to their personal characteristics, their intellectual force, and their methods.

Without disparaging the powers of observation of some who have undertaken to analyze or to delineate the characters of the Big Four, I cannot but feel amazement at their emphatic statements, which, so far as actual knowledge is concerned, are based upon three or four casual interviews with these statesmen, and not upon frequent intercourse with them. Evidently such writers build their opinions chiefly on hearsay and very little on actual knowledge. It is manifest that their appreciation is superficial and should be so recognized by those who are critical in their study of personality. If the knowledge of these authors were equal to the positiveness of their assertions, their

Introduction

word portraits would be almost priceless. The danger lies in the possibility that future generations, assuming that their judgments are drawn from sufficient personal observations, may accept their writings as true and accurate likenesses of those whom they purport to describe, when, in fact, the prejudice and fancy of common gossip have much to do with their tone and color. In truth, the descriptions of these leaders at Paris which have appeared from time to time have been a chief inducement for me to write these sketches.

In order that the comments upon the negotiations at Paris which appear in the succeeding pages may not be misconstrued, or relied upon to justify those who have opposed a speedy ratification of the Treaty of Versailles, it may be proper to say that, defective as the treaty is in certain particulars, nevertheless, considering that it had gone as far as it had and that the supreme need of the world was an immediate restoration of a state of peace, the situation demanded, in my judgment, its signature and should have secured its prompt ratification by the United States. To have declined to sign the treaty and by doing so to have delayed the peace would, as it seemed

Introduction

at the time, have jeopardized the political and social order in many European countries, and the same peril seemed to arise from the withholding of senatorial consent to the ratification of the treaty.

Whatever criticisms may be justly made of the conduct of the negotiations at Paris and however sound may be some of the objections raised as to the terms of the Treaty of Versailles, they appeared in the summer of 1919 insufficient grounds to warrant the refusal to sign or ratify the document. In 1919 there was an almost universal belief that a restoration of peace was imperative. It was then paramount to every other consideration. Even if American interests were adversely affected, the Constitution of the United States seemed to give ample protection from the treaty obligations which were considered to be contrary to America's traditional policies. As President Wilson had definitely made up his mind not to accept any actual modifications of the articles in the treaty relating to the League of Nations, the only expedient course seemed to be to obtain ratification without change of the articles if peace was to be restored prior to 1920.

Introduction

When, however, the Senate declined to give its consent to ratification without substantial reservations, and when President Wilson declared that the covenant of the League of Nations should be made an issue in the presidential campaign of 1920 and that the election should be considered a solemn referendum of the people of the United States as to its acceptance, the chief argument for urging ratification without change disappeared. If peace was to be postponed until the popular will was expressed at the polls in November, 1920, then it was proper and advisable to consider the rejection of the covenant or amendments and reservations to it which would cure its fundamental defects. With an immediate peace out of the question, revision of the articles seemed wise, as before their acceptance without revision had seemed wise and for the best interests of the nations.

I

CLEMENCEAU

OF the four heads of states M. Clemenceau, the president of the Peace Conference, was, in my judgment, the dominant figure and the strongest man of the many strong men who participated in the negotiations at Paris. Possibly his age, which in no way impaired his keenness of wit or vigor of address, his long and turbulent political career, and the courage and firmness which he had shown during the perils of the German offensive in May, June, and July, 1918, had much to do with the impression which he made upon me. But without the background of accomplishment M. Clemenceau possessed a strength of character and a forcefulness which would have raised him above his colleagues. Persistent though patient, he was always ready, when the moment arrived, to use all his skill and cleverness in debate to obtain a decision which would be in the interest of his country. Every question was viewed by him in the light of how it would affect France. He was supremely nationalistic and interpreted international adjustments into na-

Clemenceau

tional terms. To advance French interests was
his dominant purpose.

When President Wilson arrived in France
about the middle of December, 1918, and was
everywhere received with unparalleled enthusiasm by the people, who believed him to be the
apostle of human rights and the uncompromising
champion of a just peace, M. Clemenceau doubtless witnessed the ovations accorded the President with a measure of uncertainty as to the man
who was thus idolized and who so manifestly had
the confidence of the French people. Essentially
practical, he looked forward, I imagine, to the
time when these first outbursts of enthusiasm
would subside and the popular mind would become more normal. The shrewd old statesman,
familiar from long experience with every phase
of the emotional French nature, and knowing the
impatience and instability of popular favor, must
have realized that the American leader could not,
unless he was indeed the superman many thought
him to be, continue to hold the high place in
public confidence which he had attained by his
declarations as to the fundamentals of peace and
by his spectacular arrival in Paris with the un-
doubted purpose of forcing their acceptance.

Clemenceau

Judging from the course of events it is not improbable that M. Clemenceau deliberately delayed organizing the work of the Conference until he had an opportunity to learn more of the character and ability of Mr. Wilson. He knew Mr. Lloyd George and Signor Orlando, but the President was practically unknown to him except through his public utterances. Possibly, too, he did not wish to have the Conference meet until the Supreme War Council met on January 11th to extend the armistice, as it would form an easy stepping-stone for him to assume a general direction of the proceedings.

It was not difficult to cause this delay, because the machinery for arranging the preliminaries was entirely in the hands of the French, as the meeting-place was Paris. It was a foregone conclusion and in accord with international custom that the Secretary General and most of his active assistants would be French and that M. Clemenceau would be able through them to control the proceedings after the Conference was organized. The customary practice would have been for a Frenchman to preside over the Conference, but the presence of President Wilson as a delegate raised a question as to the propriety of any

other than the President of the French Republic
presiding, and under the system of responsible
government in France M. Poincaré was not acceptable as a delegate, since he was not fully in
harmony with the policies of the Clemenceau
ministry. I have an impression that Mr. Wilson
had the idea that he would be asked to preside
over the Conference and act *ex officio* as chairman
of the committee, commission, or council which
would direct the proceedings. But if he was
disappointed when this honor went to another,
he never showed that he was, accepting the
situation with perfect equanimity, and, in fact,
nominating M. Clemenceau for the presidency.

M. Clemenceau had at the outset perceived
that if the President did not sit as a delegate, he
would exercise a dominant influence over the
negotiations and be in a measure the final arbiter
of disputed questions. The natural step, therefore, was to deprive the President of this superior
position by inducing him to sit at the peace table
as one of the American delegation, thereby
putting him on the same level as the other heads
of states present at the Conference. For two or
three weeks after the Americans arrived in Paris,
M. Clemenceau, aided by his colleagues, exerted

his powers of persuasion to obtain the President's consent to act as a delegate. I do not know the arguments used or inducements offered, but, whatever they were, they succeeded, although the President remained long undecided, and acceded, I believe, with hesitation, if not with reluctance, to their wishes.

Having persuaded the President to assume a position which placed him on a level with the premiers of the Entente Powers and entitled him to no greater consideration than they received in the conduct of the proceedings, M. Clemenceau could, according to international usage, become the President of the Conference. This he did with the same tact and shrewdness that he had shown in inducing the President to become a delegate.

When it became necessary to arrange the terms for extending the armistice with Germany, which expired in January, the Supreme War Council was summoned to meet with the Military Council, on the 12th of the month, at the Ministry of Foreign Affairs. Over this body M. Clemenceau had in the past presided, and he assumed the chair as a matter of course. When the terms of renewing the armistice were settled, questions pertaining to the Conference were taken up and the number of delegates to be allotted to each country represented was determined, as well as the continued control of the proceedings by the Council. Thus without an interruption in the session, except by the withdrawal of the military chieftains, the Supreme War Council was converted into the Council of Ten, and M. Clemenceau continued to preside without any question being raised as to the propriety of his doing so. In fact, no opportunity was offered to object had there been a disposition to make the subject an issue.

But besides giving M. Clemenceau a superior place in directing the proceedings, this transformation of the War Council into the Council of Ten established the policy that the five principal Powers were to have directing control over the Conference and its deliberations. Thus the French Premier gained three points especially advantageous to his country: the oligarchy of the Five Powers, in which France would be influential on account of her military strength; a dominant voice in the Council of Ten through the chairmanship; and direction of the programme and proceedings of the Conference and Council by means of the Secretariat General.

Clemenceau

The calmness and ease with which M. Clemenceau carried through the plan to hold the management of the negotiations in his own hands and his skillful utilization of a unique state of affairs to that end suggest the movements of a well-oiled piece of machinery. Without noise and without apparent friction he assumed the chairmanship and subordinated the other heads of delegations to less prominent positions, and this in spite of the popular opinion as to the superior qualities of President Wilson and as to the place he should have in the assembled congress of the nations.

Once in the saddle, Clemenceau, contrary to the public estimate of his nature, did not ride roughshod over his colleagues. As the presiding officer of the Council of Ten his conduct was urbane and considerate, although I cannot say the same of him when he presided over the Conference on the Preliminaries of Peace, a position which he assumed with the same assurance with which he had assumed the presidency of the Council. In dealing with the great body of delegates, which met usually in the Salle de l'Horloge of the Palace of the Ministry of Foreign Affairs, he lived up to his reputation. He was,

in fact, utterly ruthless in pressing through the
programme agreed upon by the Council of Ten.
He swept aside objections and suppressed interruptions with little regard for the speakers who
dared to challenge his will. The way he forced
business forward, ignoring or rebuking a delegate
whom he thought opposed to the programme, reminded one of the methods frequently employed
at an American ward caucus a generation ago.
His caustic sentences, his fluency of speech, increasing in vehemence as he proceeded, and his
real or assumed passion simply overwhelmed
protest and resistance. It was in such manifestations of fiery temper and intensity of purpose
that one understood how the old statesman had
won his *nom politique*, *Le Tigre*.

No one who attended a plenary session of the
Conference on the Preliminaries of Peace can
ever forget M. Clemenceau as he stood with head
thrown back between his broad, humped shoulders, with the knuckles of his gray-gloved hands
resting on the green table in front of him, and
with his thick, shaggy brows drawn partially
over his dark eyes, which fairly sparkled as he
addressed the delegates. He usually began
speaking in a deliberate and rather monotonous

voice, but with no hesitation or break in the even flow of his words. As he proceeded, he became more and more emphatic, while the rapidity of his utterance increased until it suggested the drumming of a machine gun. He had none of the arts of oratory, but his distinct and incisive delivery compelled attention if not applause. He seemed to hurl his words at his listeners. Only occasionally did he employ a gesture, but, when he did, it was vigorous and wholly French. Having finished a forceful address, he either sank back panting into his great golden chair, or, if he desired to check further debate, he would state the resolution or decision agreed upon by the Council of Ten before the session, and without a moment's delay exclaim, *"Adopté."* He would then, before any one could interrupt, take up the next item on the agenda, or else add, *"Ajourné."*

Free debate and actual voting by the delegates had no place in the proceedings with M. Clemenceau in the chair. There was an occasional attempt at discussion, but the Clemenceau method discouraged it. After listening with a tolerant manner and with his half-closed eyes turned toward the ceiling, the old French auto-

crat would slowly rise from his chair, glare
fiercely about the room as if to say, " We have
had enough of this," and ask whether any one
else desired to speak; and then, before another
delegate could collect his wits and get to his feet,
he would snap out the inevitable *"Adopté."*
That always ended it.

This procedure was the easier because the
assembled delegates knew that the proposed
measures which appeared on the agenda or were
read by the President of the Conference or the
Secretary General had been considered and ap-
proved by the Council of Ten before being sub-
mitted. In the face of this united approval of the
Five Great Powers opposition crumbled. The
possibility of offending the ruling oligarchy or the
futility of attempting to reverse their decisions
caused most of the delegates to remain silent. A
few, more courageous than their fellows, such as
Hymans, of Belgium, Bratiano, of Rumania, and·
Hughes, of Australia, dared to speak their minds
until the Old Tiger showed his teeth and growled
out, *"Adopté."* Then they, too, succumbed.

Altogether a plenary session of the Conference
on the Preliminaries of Peace was a farce. It was
never a deliberative assembly which reached an

agreement by a frank exchange of views. The delegates were called together to listen, not to criticize or object, to the programme of the Council of Ten. They were there to go through the formality of registering their approval, whatever their real opinions might be. It was medieval rather than modern; despotic rather than democratic. It was in one sense a farce, but in another it was a tragedy.

To carry through a proceeding of this sort required a masterful man like M. Clemenceau. President Wilson could never have done it. Even his nature, which resents opposition, would have found such methods repugnant to his sense of right and fair play. I doubt if Mr. Lloyd George could have done it. But M. Clemenceau suffered from no qualms of indecision. His fixed determination and driving force were just the qualities needful to crush opposition and to compel submission. He drove toward the goal, heedless of the obstacles in the way, and supremely confident in his ability to attain the object sought. These were the characteristics which made him the great War Minister of France even when the German hosts, flushed with successes, were sweeping toward Paris. These were the charac-

teristics which gained him the applause of the
world and the adoration of the French people.
It is no exaggeration to say that in the dark days
of 1918 the indomitable courage and stern will
of M. Clemenceau were the greatest assets of
France, for the fire of his spirit ran through the
nation, inspiring confidence and determination.
But these characteristics, of so great value during
the war, were the ones which he unfortunately
employed as President of the Conference. They
succeeded, but the success was at a sacrifice
which was far too great.

M. Clemenceau, the believer in the primacy of
the Great Powers, which he succeeded in putting
into practical operation in the Council of Ten,
and even more completely in the Council of Four,
saw with satisfaction the same idea perpetuated
in the Council of the League of Nations. To
be the executive of such an oligarchy in the Peace
Conference he was specially equipped by experience, by temperament, and by resourcefulness.
His nature was that of a despot.

I imagine that he viewed the sessions of the
Conference as expedient in order to satisfy the
sentimental idea that every nation which had
actually participated in the war against Germany

should have a voice in making peace, but he determined that the voices of the small belligerents should be merely echoes of the expressed will of the Great Powers. He manifestly believed that those who possessed the superior military and naval strength had the sole right to make peace with the Central Alliance. He did not propose to hazard the interests of France by submitting the treaty terms to the body of delegates for decision. Having won the war, he did not intend to have France lose the peace.

Skeptical as M. Clemenceau seemed to be of the actual force of moral obligation and of abstract justice in international relations, he conceived that the practical way was for the five principal Powers to take and keep entire control of the negotiations and to perpetuate their control by means of a concert of the Great Powers, or, if it made any one happier, by a Council of a League of Nations, which was the same thing if it recognized the primacy of the Five Powers. In my judgment that is what M. Clemenceau sought from the beginning, and that is what he obtained. Less far-seeing than he and less appreciative of the great advantages to France of the creation of such an oligarchy, the

military element in France, led by Marshal Foch
and his political friends, were insistent on making
the Rhine the boundary with Germany, the Marshal even going so far as to denounce the treaty
in a plenary session because this provision was
not included. But M. Clemenceau knew that the
unity of the Great Powers was a stronger protection to his country than the military occupation
of territory whose inhabitants would remain
hostile and seek the first opportunity to throw off
the yoke of French sovereignty. He knew that
if he insisted on the Foch programme it would
result in the loss of the unity which he desired
and would greatly weaken the influence of France
in the Council of the Powers. Wisdom and expediency from the French point of view endorsed
the course taken by the French Premier. He
endeavored nevertheless to remove all popular
opposition aroused by the militarists by negotiating treaties of protective alliance with the
United States and Great Britain, but in this he
was only partially successful, as the extreme
militarists continued their demand for the cession
of the territory west of the Rhine in spite of the
treaties.

It is not my purpose to repeat the opinions of

the delegates of small nations concerning the organization and procedure of the Peace Conference and the way M. Clemenceau conducted the plenary sessions. It is enough to say that they were astonished, indignant, and depressed at their treatment, but dared not publicly complain of their wrongs, though in private their bitterness was expressed in strong terms. The invectives were chiefly directed against M. Clemenceau because of his " brutal and unheard-of conduct " as President of the Conference, though they must have known that he was only the instrument of the arbitrary power which had been taken over by the Councils. The resentment of the delegates increased as weeks lengthened into months while they sat idly cooling their heels and awaiting the decrees of the Great Powers. Having no alternative they assented when they were told to assent, and they also signed when they were directed to sign, the Chinese delegates alone refusing to place their signatures to the treaty of peace. It was a succession of humiliations for the independent states, whose delegates sat at the peace table presumably to register the sovereign wills of their respective nations, but in fact to obey the commands of the Great Pow-

ers under the direction of the forceful old statesman of France. It is true that these nations were
represented on various commissions, but the commissions possessed no authority to decide a question. That authority rested with the Councils.

But Clemenceau presiding over the Council of
Ten was a different Clemenceau from him who
presided over the plenary sessions of the Conference on the Preliminaries of Peace. The Council,
except on rare occasions when there were a great
number of military and naval experts present,
met in the room occupied as an office by
M. Pichon, the French Minister of Foreign Affairs.
On the south side of this room wide windows,
extending from the floor to the lofty ceiling,
looked out upon the trees and shrubbery of a
small court. The three other sides were cov-
ered above the dark wainscoting with richly
colored tapestries, which in allegory portrayed
events in the life of Henry IV. In the center of
the north side two sets of double doors opened
into one of the large antechambers facing the
Quai d'Orsay. The doors on the inside of the
thick wall were connected by brass rods with
corresponding doors on the outer side, so that
the two opened together. When they were closed,

Clemenceau

M. Pichon's room was practically sound-proof.

The council chamber was approximately thirty feet from east to west and over twenty feet wide. Near the western end and several feet from a handsome fireplace, in which a wood fire blazed on cold days, was M. Pichon's ornate desk, or rather table. At this sat M. Clemenceau in a low-backed armchair. Behind him Professor Mantoux, the gifted interpreter of the Conference, sat at a small table. Near Professor Mantoux and toward the south side of the room sat M. Pichon in a high-backed armchair. Along the south side of the room were the other members of the Council, with their backs to the windows, arranged in the following order — the Americans, the British, the Italians, and the Japanese. They sat in great chairs similar to that occupied by M. Pichon, and had in front of them small tables for their papers and maps. Behind the members of the Council, in the embrasures of the windows and also along the east side of the room, were their secretaries and the expert advisers whom they had asked to attend the session. On the north side near the western end of the room sat M. Dutasta, the Secretary General, and three or four French assistants. Also on the north side close to the entrance doors were chairs for delegates, commissioners, and other persons who might be summoned to present their cases or make their reports to the Council. As a rule from twenty to thirty-five people were present at each session, though on occasions all retired except the ten members.

This is a rude picture of the place of meeting of the Council of Ten over which M. Clemenceau presided. But, as I said, he was a different man from the man who directed the proceedings of a plenary session. Within the council chamber his domineering manner, his brusqueness of speech, and his driving methods of conducting business disappeared. He showed patience and consideration toward his colleagues and seldom spoke until the others had expressed their views. It was only on rare occasions that he abandoned his suavity of address and allowed his emotions to affect his utterances. It was then only that one caught a glimpse of the ferocity of The Tiger. But these incidents were very unusual, as M. Clemenceau was generally conciliatory and disposed to find some common ground for compromise. His manifest purpose was to obtain unanimity by mutual concessions.

Clemenceau

After a long debate, in which several members of the Council had taken part, M. Clemenceau would turn to the one who had offered the original proposal and ask expectantly in English, "Do you agree?" If the proposer showed that he was not satisfied, M. Clemenceau would gaze at the ceiling and patiently listen to further discussion. If it became apparent that no agreement could be reached, he would ask for suggestions as to the course to be taken. If, however, the author of the proposal was satisfied with the changes offered in debate, M. Clemenceau would put the same question to others who had taken part in the discussion, and if no objection was raised his face would light up and he would exclaim, "*Bien! C'est adopté.*" It was then the duty of the Secretary General and the secretaries of the delegations to reduce the final decision to writing, by no means an easy task if it was a patchwork of debate.

The proceedings of the Council of Ten were very informal, although an official agenda was prepared for each session, nominally by the secretaries acting together, though in fact it was done by M. Dutasta in consultation with officials of the French Foreign Office. Thus M. Clemen-

ceau and his advisers substantially regulated
the subjects discussed by the Council of Ten.
The truth is that the agenda seldom reached the
members of the Council long enough before the
session for them to study thoroughly or in detail
the subjects listed for discussion. Naturally this
gave a decided advantage to the French, who
included in the agenda only subjects which they
were fully prepared to discuss. It was practically
impossible to have placed on the agenda a subject which officials of the French Foreign Office
were not ready to consider or which they believed
it would be for the interests of France to postpone
until certain other matters had been decided.

Of course M. Clemenceau, alive to everything
which worked to the advantage of France and
skillful in handling situations of all sorts,
succeeded in carrying through the French programme; and he did it without exciting opposition among his colleagues. They might and, in a
few cases, did grumble and complain outside the
Council as to the way matters were being
handled, but in M. Pichon's room the suavity,
good nature, and unfailing courtesy of The Tiger
silenced those who were dissatisfied. In the
endeavor to match the shrewd old statesman in

politeness and geniality they failed to use these qualities in the way that he did. He used them to disarm his opponents and prevent vigorous objection. His colleagues used them to soften the blows which they intended to deliver. M. Clemenceau won.

As a master of the fine art of flattery none could equal the French Premier. It was interesting to see how accurately he estimated the personal peculiarities of his colleagues and how tactfully he regulated his intercourse accordingly. With President Wilson he was, at least in the Council of Ten, politely deferential, but never subservient; with Mr. Lloyd George he showed his wit and sometimes his sarcasm; with the Italians he was cynical and caustic and not infrequently vehement; and with the Japanese, indifferent or patiently tolerant. He had read with remarkable keenness the temperament and the characteristics of each, and seemed to understand the best way to deal with each one.

The personality of M. Clemenceau was distinctly attractive. His genial friendliness, his mental alertness, and his sparkling wit made him always an agreeable companion and an interesting conversationalist. It is true that his wit was sometimes biting and cruel. He did not check his fondness for uttering clever sayings because they conveyed unpleasant truths or wounded the sensibilities of those at whom they were directed. But he was always careful to avoid offending one whose power he recognized or whose favor he sought. President Wilson, for example, was never in my presence a target for his sarcastic remarks, while his own officials and military advisers, even Marshal Foch, were often the subjects of jests and rebukes which, delivered before the Council, caused them exceeding mortification and invited in some cases angry retorts. He was at times so harsh and sarcastic in his language that his listeners felt incensed that he took an occasion when they were present to humiliate his subordinates.

Yet in spite of these exhibitions of temper, embarrassing as they were, one could not but admire the sturdy old veteran, whose political life had been one of continual tumult and strife. No public man in France had had so stormy a career as he. He had not won his high place by making friends with politicians; he had won it by trampling down his enemies. He did not owe his success to a political party or to a faction; he

Clemenceau

owed it to compelling recognition of his personal strength and ability. He simply reveled in the struggles in which he was constantly engaged to maintain his position. He never hesitated to pick up a gage of battle, and he entered the conflict with all the vigor of youth and all the sagacity of age.

Whatever may be thought of M. Clemenceau's policies and methods, it is impossible to deny tribute to his indomitable will and his unwavering optimism as he stood alone and defiant during many of the crises which he as Premier was called upon to face. Even those who disliked him intensely could not refuse him unwilling praise for his devotion and service to France, while the enthusiastic shouts of "Clemenceau! Clemenceau!" whenever he appeared in public, testified to a popularity which silenced his enemies and made his premiership secure.

I cannot better describe M. Clemenceau's personal appearance than to say that he suggested in face and figure a Chinese mandarin of the old empire. I say this with all respect for the man whom I would describe. He had the sallow complexion, the prominent high cheek-bones, the massive forehead with protuberant brows, the

slant of the dark eyes, the long, down-curving
gray mustache, the short neck, the broad,
rounded shoulders, and the bulky body. As he
sat in the council chamber with his clenched
gloved hands resting on the arms of his chair, his
eyes with their raised brows and heavy, drooping
lids, and his features immobile and expression-
less, he might have been the model for a bronze
Chinese statue of Buddha. He was a striking
type, indicative of intellectual force, of self-
mastery, and of cold, merciless will power.
Massive, Mongolian, and impassive, he watched
the course of events with Oriental stoicism and
calculated with the unerring instinct of the Western mind where lay the interests of France, to
which his thought and energies were consecrated.

It is not strange or doubtful, when one dissects
the character of this remarkable man, that he
dominated the Peace Conference and the Councils at Paris. He possessed the essential qualities
of great leadership. He knew when to be defiant
and when to placate. He was preëminently
practical and material. He was cynical of the
real value of the idealism which had been so
widely applauded and which many of the delegates supported with enthusiasm so long as it did

not interfere with the material interests of their
countries. He tolerated these ideals because it
was the expedient thing to do. He showed, in
what he sought and in what he accomplished
rather than in what he said, that he believed that
selfishness was the supreme impulse with nations
as with individuals, and that it was the only real
factor to be reckoned with. Altruism was well
enough to talk about because it was pleasing to
some people, but to construct international society on such a foundation was to deny human
nature. He was in no sense a visionary.

The League of Nations to M. Clemenceau — if
I read his mind correctly — was a Utopian dream
of impractical theorists, until a concert of the
Great Powers was incorporated in the covenant
and the United States and Great Britain agreed
to enter into treaties to come to the aid of France
in the event that Germany should again attack
her. From the time that these treaties of protection were arranged, and his country had no
longer to depend for its security upon the uncertain guaranty of the covenant, M. Clemenceau supported, or rather did not oppose, the
League of Nations. He probably thought that it
might have some practical uses in carrying out

Clemenceau

the terms of the treaty. If the authors and sponsors wished to try out their theory, he had no objections, provided there was nothing in the covenant which weakened or lessened the material advantages obtained for France in the terms of the peace.

He watched calmly and with little comment the formulation of the League by the Commission on the League of Nations, over which President Wilson presided, but I imagine that he did so with a scornful cynicism for the work of those who, he doubtless thought, were wasting their time on a dream. Had the authors of the covenant attempted, however, to modify his purposes, there can be little doubt that there would have been an explosion and the covenant would have had a difficult road to travel before it was accepted.

His fixity of purpose, his practicality, his tolerance of harmless altruism, his mental vitality and keenness of perception, together with the other traits of character to which I have referred, made M. Clemenceau the most influential personality in the Paris Conference. He succeeded in nearly everything that he undertook. When it made no difference to France or to

Clemenceau

French interests, he might argue and debate and finally give up the point; but if the real interests of France, as he saw them, were in the slightest degree affected, he never surrendered. His patriotism like his materialism was extreme. No one can honestly deny the superior influence which the rugged old statesman exerted from first to last over his distinguished confrères.

II

WILSON

For obvious reasons it is harder for me to analyze the character of President Wilson as manifested in his conduct at Paris than it is the character of any one of his colleagues in the Council of the Heads of States. It was only as I reviewed the results of the negotiations that I came to a realization of the difficulty, if not the impossibility, of harmonizing his avowed intentions with what seemed to satisfy him. As a consequence, in a character study of this sort, the facts do not always seem to justify the conclusions. Then, too, opinion is often based on deductions which depend more upon impressions than on direct evidence. I may have drawn erroneous conclusions and may therefore be wrong in my judgments; that I am willing to admit; but it is my earnest purpose to be entirely impartial and to avoid any personal bias in the discussion of a man with whom I was so long and so closely associated.

A real difficulty in portraying President Wilson

as he was in Paris is that certain traits of his character, which had been so prominent in his public career prior to that time, seem to have been suppressed or submerged in the new environment. Whether this was intentional or involuntary I do not know; and really it makes no difference. The fact is that the President appeared changed after he landed in France. Clearly it is difficult not to be unconsciously influenced by impressions gained prior to the Paris days and not to weave those memories into an estimate of Mr. Wilson when he was engaged in the task of negotiating the terms of the treaty of peace with Germany.

It is not my purpose to discuss the wisdom of the President's attending the Peace Conference and of conducting in person the negotiations. As to that there will always be, I presume, a divergence of opinion. There are valid arguments on both sides of the question. I can only say that the day after the armistice was signed, I had a conference with the President in his study at the White House, during which I took occasion to tell him that in my judgment it would be a serious mistake for him to sit at the peace table, and I went fully into my reasons for so advising

Harris & Ewing, Washington, D.C.

Wilson

him. Six days later — November 18, 1918 — the
President came to my residence and told me that,
after considering the matter very carefully, he
had determined to go to the Conference, and had
given out a public announcement of his intention.
My judgment as to the President's personal participation in the negotiations and his absence
from the United States for so long a period is the
same now as it was the day I expressed it. I
leave others to decide how far it has been justified
by subsequent events. At the same time I wish
to show that the President's decision to exercise
in person his constitutional right to conduct the
foreign affairs of the United States was not the
result of impulse, but was reached after thought-
ful deliberation, and doubtless the manifestations of approval by the French people of his
presence at Paris convinced him that he had
decided wisely.

No man ever received a more demonstrative
welcome than did Mr. Wilson from the moment
that the George Washington entered the harbor
of Brest. It was a great popular ovation. His
name was on every lip; throngs of admirers
applauded him as he entered the special train for
Paris, and at the stations *en route;* and multi-

tudes, delirious with enthusiasm, cheered him a
welcome as he drove through the beflagged
streets of the French capital in company with
President Poincaré, who met him at the Gare du
Bois de Boulogne. It was a reception which
might have turned the head of a man far less
responsive than the President was to public applause, and have given him an exalted opinion
of his own power of accomplishment and of his
individual responsibility to mankind. It is fair,
I think, to assume that this was the effect on
the President. It was the natural one.

This convincing evidence of his personal popularity, which was vastly increased by his subsequent visits to London and Rome, doubtless
confirmed him in the belief that, with the people
of the three principal Allied Powers so unani-
mously behind him, the statesmen of those
countries would hardly dare to oppose his ideas
as to the terms of peace. I think that there were
ample grounds for this belief.

The trouble was that the President was not
prepared to seize the opportunity and to capital-
ize this general popular support. He came to
Paris without, so far as I know, a definite outline
of a treaty with Germany. He did have a draft

of a covenant of a league of nations, but it was a crude and undigested plan, as is evident by a comparison of it with the document finally reported to the Conference on the Preliminaries of Peace. He, of course, had his famous Fourteen Points, and the declarations appearing in his subsequent addresses as bases of the peace, but they were little more than a series of principles and policies to guide in the drafting of actual terms. As to a complete *projet*, or even an outline of terms which could be laid before the delegates for consideration, he apparently had none; in fact when this lack was felt by members of the American Commission they undertook to have their legal advisers prepare a skeleton treaty, but had to abandon the work after it was well under way because the President resented the idea, asserting emphatically that he did not intend to allow lawyers to draw the treaty, a declaration that discouraged those of the profession from volunteering suggestions as to the covenant and other articles of the treaty. The President, not having done the preliminary work himself, and unwilling to have others do it, was wholly unprepared to submit anything in concrete form to the European statesmen, unless it was his imperfect plan for a league of nations. The consequence was that the general scheme of the treaty and many of the important articles were prepared and worked out by the British and French delegations. Thus the exceptional opportunity which the President had to impress his ideas on the Conference, and to lead in the negotiations, was lost, and he failed to maintain his controlling position among the statesmen who were, as it turned out, to dictate the terms of peace; while his utterances, which had been the foundation of his popularity, suffered in a measure the same fate.

If the President had adopted the customary method of negotiation through commissioners instead of pursuing the unusual and in fact untried method of personal participation, the situation would have been very different. Without the President present in Paris detailed instructions would have been prepared, which could have been modified during the negotiations only by reference to him at Washington. Instructions of that sort would of necessity have been definite. There would have been no uncertainty as to the objects sought. But with the President on the ground written instructions

Wilson

seemed to him, and possibly were, superfluous. He was there to decide the attitude of the United States and to give oral directions concerning the minutest detail of the negotiations as the questions arose; and since diplomatic commissioners are in any event only agents of the President and subject always to his instructions, the American commissioners at Paris possessed no right to act independently or to do other than follow the directions which they received, which in this case were given by word of mouth. As these directions were meager and indefinite, and as they did not include a general plan, the situation was unsatisfactory and embarrassing for the President's American colleagues.

I doubt if Mr. Wilson had worked out, even tentatively, the application of the principles and precepts which he had declared while the war was in progress, and which had been generally accepted at the time of the armistice as the bases of peace. The consequence was that he must have had a very vague and nebulous scheme for their introduction into the treaty, because many of his declarations required accurate definition before they could be practically applied to the problems which awaited solution by the Conference. Naturally there was an atmosphere of uncertainty and a feeling of helplessness in approaching the treaty terms which prevented the American commissioners from pressing for definite objects. The whole delegation, the President included, lost prestige and influence with the foreign delegates by this lack of a programme.

Here is shown one of the inherent weaknesses of Mr. Wilson which impaired his capacity as the head of a diplomatic commission to negotiate so intricate 'a settlement as the treaty with Germany. He was inclined to let matters drift, relying apparently on his own quickness of perception and his own sagacity to defeat or amend terms proposed by members of other delegations. From first to last there was no teamwork, no common counsel, and no concerted action. It was discouraging to witness this utter lack of system, when system was so essential. The reason was manifest. There was no directing head to the American Commission to formulate a plan, to organize the work and to issue definite instructions.

It is my belief that this fault in the conduct of the negotiations, so far as the United States is concerned, was responsible in no small degree for some of the more undesirable settlements which were incorporated in the treaty of peace. The other heads of states held long daily conferences with their fellow commissioners and principal expert advisers, at which pending questions were debated at length and opinions were freely expressed as to the attitude which should be assumed in view of the national interests involved. Not so the President. He seldom met the American commissioners as a body — in fact, only nine times prior to his first return to the United States on February 14th—and then, except in regard to the covenant, the discussions were desultory and of a general character except on two or three occasions. The President at these meetings did most of the talking, seldom asking advice. They left an impression of doubt as to just what he was seeking to obtain. They might have been, but were not, useful. During the entire period of the negotiations President Wilson summoned the experts to meet as a body with the American Commission only once, on June 3d, when the German and Austrian treaties were completed.

The President's method of utilizing the knowledge of others was this: If he wished advice he called on the individual whom he thought especially qualified to give it — though he sometimes erred in his choice — and discussed the subject with him in a private interview, or else he asked the expert to prepare for him a confidential memorandum. The result of the interview the President did not disclose, but the commissioners sometimes obtained from the adviser an oral account of what took place or a copy of the memorandum which he had furnished. There was, therefore, no consensus of opinion by the commission, and no general discussion of a question. The President, in fact, constituted himself an exclusive repository of all information, opinions, and speculations, to which no one else had access. It was entirely a personal matter with him. It seems to me to be a fair assumption that he argued that, as he alone had the responsibility under the Constitution, it was for him to make up his mind independently as to the course which should be taken, and that it was time enough to tell the other American commissioners what that course would be after he had determined it. Unfortunately, he did not always disclose his decision even when he reached one, though on more than one occasion he seemed surprised that his colleagues were ignorant of his views, which they could have gained only by intuition or in some cases by deduction.

The aloofness of Mr. Wilson, his apparent dislike for consultations until circumstances made them unavoidable, and his manifest desire and purpose to remain isolated were not new traits in his character. They had been recognized and not infrequently commented upon long before we went to Paris, but the circumstances surrounding an international conference of such magnitude as the Peace Conference and the imperative need of close personal intercourse between associates in the conduct of the negotiations emphasized these peculiarities of the President's nature and seriously handicapped the activities of the American commissioners.

The foregoing consideration of the President's relations to the other American commissioners explains in a large measure the reason for his failure to retain the first place in the Conference, which he undoubtedly held when he first arrived in France. He was unable to avail himself of the opportunity offered by his unique position because of this defect in his mental attitude toward coöperation. Though he frequently sought the advice of Colonel House, at least during the early stages of the negotiations, he remained a solitary and secluded man, preferring to bear his burdens alone.

The consequences were those which might have been expected. M. Clemenceau, and in a lesser degree Mr. Lloyd George, took the initiative on practically all subjects requiring settlement except as to those before commissions of the Conference, and even in the case of the Commission on the League of Nations, of which the President was the presiding officer, the initiative apparently passed from him to General Smuts and Lord Robert Cecil. Thus the United States was forced into the position of following instead of leading in the drafting of the terms formulated in the Council of Four, a position which was as unnecessary as it was unfortunate.

There can be little doubt that President Wilson expected to find in the principal statesmen of Europe, at least in a measure, the same philanthropic and altruistic motives which he possessed to so high a degree. In the correspondence during the war the Allies had responded to his appeals and declarations in a tone of lofty idealism similar to that which he had used. I believe that he assumed that moral right would be the controlling factor in the settlements at Paris, and that even the enemy would be treated fairly, if not generously, in order that the peace might be erected on permanent foundations. Entertaining idealistic motives and unfortunately lacking practical experience in international negotiations, the President did not appear to appreciate at the first that the aims of his foreign colleagues were essentially material or to realize that their expressions of high principle were merely an assent to a moral standard which they thought basicly right, but at present impracticable. The result was that he assented to certain arrangements before he became aware of the selfishness, if not the greed, which was so evidently a frequent impulse of many of the European delegates in formulating their demands or supporting those of others. Having once passed his word in regard to a decision, his high sense of honor or possibly an unwillingness to admit his error prevented him from withdrawing it.

Obsessed with the idea that the organization of a league of nations was the supreme object to be attained at the Paris Conference, the President devoted his time, his effort, and his influence to drafting its charter and removing or neutralizing the objections which stood in the way of its acceptance. At the first he conferred with the other American commissioners in regard to the covenant, but on finding them, except possibly Colonel House, more or less skeptical as to the practical operation of the organization which he had planned in collaboration with Lord Robert Cecil and General Smuts, and disposed to offer suggestions materially modifying the plan, he showed that he preferred only the coöperation of those who unreservedly believed in his draft. It was very apparent that he did not desire counsel and criticism, but approval and commendation of the covenant. It was unfortunate for the President and for the League that he took this attitude, as subsequent events proved.

As the leaders of the Allied Powers, with their practical ideas, came to a realization of the situation and saw that the President was willing to concede much in exchange for support of the covenant, they utilized his supreme desire to obtain by barter material advantages for their own nations. From the results of the negotiations it may be deduced that by clever representations they gained concession after concession. The

Wilson

apparent support of the idealism of the President
by these statesmen was in my opinion chiefly for
a purpose and not out of conviction. They loudly
applauded the President's declarations of principle as the just bases of peace, but they never
once attempted to apply them unless their own
national interests were advanced. They praised
the covenant as a wonderful document, as the
Magna Charta of the world, as an eternal
memorial to its author, and they subtly flattered
the President by confiding to the League every
question which could not be immediately solved,
ostensibly to show their faith in the proposed
organization, but really to postpone the settlement of dangerous disputes.

M. Clemenceau, who had frankly declared in
favor of the doctrine of the balance of power, was
satisfied with either General Smuts's plan or that
of Lord Robert Cecil, since both provided for the
perpetuation of the Supreme War Council as the
Council of the League and for the recognition of
the primacy of the Great Powers over all international affairs for the future. Mr. Lloyd
George, provided the colonial ambitions and
commercial interests of the British Empire were
satisfied before the guaranty of the covenant

became operative, complacently gave his support
to the document as a means of making more
permanent British possession of the ceded territories. Signor Orlando, assured of the dismemberment of the Austro-Hungarian Empire
and the resulting delivery into the hands of Italy
of the economic life of German Austria, and hope-
ful of being given substantial control of the
Adriatic, and confident of obtaining sovereignty
over the Tyrol by insisting on the fulfillment of
the Pact of London, rejoiced in a guaranty which
seemed to ensure, for a time at least, the widened
boundaries of Italy. The Japanese were equally
willing to unite in a mutual guaranty on con-
dition that their country obtained and was
protected in the possession of the German rights
in Shantung and in its sovereignty over the
German islands in the Pacific Ocean north of
the equator, though I am convinced that Japan
would never have withdrawn from the Conference or abandoned her position as one of the Five
Great Powers, whatever disposition had been
made of her claims.

While selfish interest undoubtedly impelled
the principal Allied Powers to adhere to the
covenant and to become members of the League

of Nations, the United States was free from such influences. It had no territorial or trade ambitions to advance. The American people desired a just peace because it would remove causes for war; they desired the creation; of an international organization which would at least hinder, if it could not actually prevent, future wars.

The ideas of the President, when he left the United States in December, 1918, were undoubtedly in general accord with the thought and desire of the majority of his countrymen as to the terms of peace. I do not mean that his plan for a league of nations, which he carried with him, but which he had not then made public, was in accord with that thought and desire. It may have been or it may not have been. No one can tell as to that. But I believe that nearly all Americans hoped and expected that some sort of an association of nations would be created at Paris. As to the form and functions of the association, public opinion in the United States had not then crystallized.

It was not until the covenant as finally reported was found to contain a mutual guaranty of territory and independence, together with

Wilson

other features which were claimed to be contrary
to American interests and to the traditional
policies of the United States, if they were not
actually violative of the Constitution, that the
President's interpretation of the popular will was
seriously questioned. When, in addition to this
opposition to the covenant,— which was seized
upon with avidity by Mr. Wilson's personal and
political enemies as an opportunity to discredit
him at home and abroad,— the injustice of
certain settlements in the treaties was manifest,
the opposition to a guaranty, which might require
coercive measures to enforce such settlements,
increased and greatly strengthened the opponents of the covenant, and in fact had much
to do with preventing the ratification of the
treaty in the Senate of the United States.

If the President had inflexibly demanded that
no terms should be written into the treaty which
were not wholly just, he would have gone far
toward accomplishing the purpose of his mission
to Europe. And if he had also advocated a plan
for a league of nations which was not open to the
charge of establishing a supernational authority,
vested to all intents in an oligarchy of the Great
Powers, he would have been acclaimed the great-

est statesman on earth. Unfortunately for the present generation and for the future peace of the world, he did not pursue this course, but distorted his declared purpose to silence opposition to his ambitious conception of a dominant international organization. The natural conclusion is that he convinced himself that the covenant as drafted could not be obtained if he insisted on complete justice in all the settlements. He chose the covenant and won support to it by compromise with those who demanded the material rewards of conquest.

The courtesy of President Wilson in greeting the members of the Council of Ten and in his intercourse with them during the sessions was unvarying. He never, so far as I can recall, showed anger or impatience. I know, however, that beneath this outward calm the President often seethed with indignation at the way matters progressed, but never by word, gesture, or change of countenance did he permit his displeasure or irritation to find open expression. He listened with greater attention to a speaker than did any other man present, and whenever opportunity offered he smiled or told an anecdote which some turn in the debate suggested. He

was invariably considerate of the expressed
opinions of others, and manifested an open mind
in valuing those opinions.

While these qualities are as a general rule useful and admirable in a negotiator, there come
times when firmness and frankness are necessary.
The failure to insist in certain cases when the
conditions of a debate required insistence lost the
President an advantage which I am sure he
would have otherwise had. Prone to postpone a
decision to the last possible moment, he puzzled
his colleagues in the Council, who could not
understand how so alert a mind needed more
time to form an opinion after listening to three
hours of discussion. This peculiarity of the
President's mental make-up was frequently
commented upon by his foreign associates in
terms by no means complimentary.

After a subject had been threshed out by the
Council of Ten, often to the point of weariness,
M. Clemenceau would often turn to the President
and ask his opinion as to the action which ought
to be taken. The President would reply without
hesitation in precise English, though he usually
evaded a decision by a general review of the
points made by both sides during the argument.

Wilson

This he did with clearness and conciseness, showing how carefully he had listened to the debate. While I think that the President's presentation showed in a way why he was not prepared to offer a solution to the question, it did not advance the work of the Council.

When the President ceased speaking, M. Clemenceau would ask my opinion, then that of Mr. Lloyd George, then that of Mr. Balfour, and so on down the line of members. He would then turn back to the President and ask, " Well, what shall we do? "

The President frequently answered, "Perhaps it would be well to refer the matter to a committee of experts "; or, "May I ask if any one has prepared a resolution? "

If the last question was asked, it was apt to bring a response from Mr. Lloyd George, whose secretaries had drafted a resolution while the discussion was in progress. A resolution laid before the Council after a question had been debated was as a rule adopted, at least in principle, though often modified in language. It was therefore a decided advantage to introduce a resolution. The President put aside this advantage by failing to suggest that the same course be taken by his expert advisers, who were naturally not disposed to follow the practice unless it was at his request. Apparently he felt an independent personal judgment by him was essential and that it would not be independent if he adopted the opinion of others. The consequence was that Mr. Lloyd George, who seldom hesitated to accept the views of his experts, introduced most of the resolutions other than those prepared by the French, which were generally annexed to the agenda.

Occasionally, however, M. Clemenceau, after a discussion in which the President had expressed definite views, would ask the latter to draft a resolution embodying his opinion. Mr. Wilson would at once take a pencil and without hesitation and without erasures write out in his small, plain hand a resolution couched with exceptional brevity in unambiguous terms. In a proposed measure of this sort the exactness of his thought and his command of language were clearly exhibited. Possessing this ability, far surpassing that of any other person attending the Council of Ten, it is all the more deplorable that he did not use it constantly. I do not recall that he prepared a resolution except at the suggestion of M. Cle-

Wilson

menceau or one of the British delegates. If he prepared one voluntarily, I do not remember the occasion. If he had done so frequently, it would have been he rather than the French or British who initiated action by the Council, and his influence over their decisions would have been marked, which in fact it was not except in a few instances.

Mr. Wilson during the sessions of the Council of Ten spoke in a low, pleasant voice and without rhetorical effort. As no one rose in speaking, he would lean forward, resting on the arms of his chair, and address his remarks first to one and then to another of his confrères. With fluency and with perfect diction he would present his views in sentences so well rounded that they suggested copper-plate perfection. His accuracy of language and his positiveness of assertion not infrequently reminded one of a lecturer imparting knowledge to a class, and gave the impression that he felt that what he said left nothing else to be said. He exhibited the traits of a philosopher rather than those of an advocate. He preferred to deal in generalities rather than with facts. His discourses, though essentially academic, were clear and logical.

Wilson

The one thing that to my mind marred the President's diction was a sort of little chuckle or half laugh which frequently interrupted his flow of language. I never observed this mannerism prior to the first meeting of the heads of states and foreign ministers except on one or two occasions. It seemed to be an involuntary act, caused by nervousness or embarrassment. It sounded almost apologetic. Probably those who had not come in frequent contact with the President prior to the Peace Conference never noticed it. To those long acquainted with him it seemed to indicate a loss of some of the assurance and self-confidence which had always been distinguishing characteristics of his public career.

After the division of the Council of Ten into the Council of the Heads of States — the Big Four — and the Council of Foreign Ministers during the last week in March, 1919, and approximately five weeks before the treaty with Germany was completed, I had little opportunity to see the President's work in conference. That he labored with great industry and took little time for rest and recreation everybody knows. He showed in his face the effect of these unremitting efforts. He looked fatigued and worn.

Wilson

Nevertheless he persisted with his characteristic determination.

The conferences of the Big Four were usually held in the palatial residence on the Place des Etats Unis, which had been provided for the President's use by the French Government. The Four generally met in the library on the ground floor, but if they had several persons present to give them advice on some technical matter, they assembled in the large salon on the second floor. At first the four statesmen met alone. Signor Orlando did not understand English, and President Wilson and Mr. Lloyd George had but an imperfect knowledge of French. M. Clemenceau was therefore the only one thoroughly familiar with both languages, and had to act as interpreter. This was found to be unsatisfactory; so Professor Mantoux was admitted, and later for some reason Sir Maurice Hankey, the secretary of the British War Mission, and also Count Aldrovandi, of the Italian Mission, were permitted to be present. Sir Maurice prepared the decisions and the minutes of the meetings. Thus the President, with no secretary present, had to depend on the notes of Hankey if any question arose as to the proceedings.

Wilson

Manifestly this was not a safe method of procedure in a negotiation which involved the national interests of different countries and dealt with many complex questions. I do not think that American interests suffered materially,— in fact, knowing the honorable character of Sir Maurice, I am sure that they did not, — but certainly the President took a needless risk in not having an American secretary present to chronicle the proceedings. It was either a failure to appreciate the importance of having his own record or else it was his inherent tendency to work alone and unaided that induced him to adopt this course, though possibly both influenced him.

President Wilson entered upon the negotiations with a high sense of honor, with altruistic purposes, and with a supreme confidence that his ideals would be written into the treaty of peace. His sense of honor and his altruism he maintained to the very end, in spite of the disappointments and discouragements resulting from the spirit of national selfishness which was so controlling in the Conference at Paris. Against this prevailing spirit the President struggled manfully. To an extent he was successful, but he not infrequently failed through the secret combinations which were formed against him. At the first his absorption in drafting and obtaining assent to the articles relating to the League of Nations caused him apparently to give but superficial consideration to other matters. Everything to his mind, as far as one could judge, depended on completing the covenant and on giving to the League an active and therefore a necessary part in carrying out the terms of settlement under the treaty. Agreements as to the settlements were apparently of secondary importance to the creation of an agency for the insurance of their performance, and the President's assent seemed to have been secured in certain cases through the menace of opposition to the covenant.

No doubt Mr. Wilson chafed under this method of negotiation,— a method as old as diplomacy itself,— feeling that he was not receiving the undivided support which he had a right to expect in his efforts to obtain a just peace. His task was arduous and exasperating. If personal toil had been the only thing, he would have been wholly successful. Had he been willing to delegate to others the negotiation of some of the decisions, important as they were, he would have had leisure to recuperate; but he was not willing. On the contrary, he insisted that everything must be decided by him, that all the threads of the treaty fabric must be in his hands. Others might help him untangle some of the knots and arrange the threads in order, but it was his business alone to weave them into the treaty. He seemed, in fact, to resent any influence exerted upon him to decide a matter in a certain way. He relied on his own judgment, and indicated that suggestion or advice, unless he requested it, was an interference with his freedom of decision and was not acceptable. Whether this attitude was the result of an abnormal conception of his constitutional responsibility for the conduct of international relations, or of an exaggerated belief in his superior mentality, I do not pretend to say.

With the multitude of decisions which had to be rendered, many of which were not only complex, but required technical knowledge of a high order, the attempt of a single individual, however gifted, to be the sole arbiter as to the proper American position in regard to them all was at the least perilous. Yet that is what the President

Wilson

tried to be. As he is entitled to credit for many
excellent provisions in the treaty because of his
steadfastness, so he cannot avoid the blame for
the questionable settlements which were inserted because he failed to object to them or else
conceded them through insufficient knowledge
or by way of compromise.

From this general comment I must exclude
the financial and economic terms of the treaty.
In the adjustment of these difficult questions
the American experts took a leading part. It
was not an easy matter to find formulæ which
would harmonize the differences between governments, each of which had its own financial and
economic interests to conserve and its own idea
as to how this could be done. That an agreement was reached, which was accepted by, if
not acceptable to, the interested parties, was a
notable accomplishment, the credit for which is
due in large measure to the Americans on the
commissions charged with the discussion and
adjustment of these conflicting interests.

What actually occurred at the meetings of
the Council of Four was unknown to the Conference as a whole. Nevertheless rumors and
reports from time to time sifted through the veil

Wilson

of secrecy which enveloped the proceedings. It
is not my purpose to discuss here the secretiveness of the Council or the impression which it
made on the delegates to the Conference and on
the public at large. Suffice it for the present
to say that the secrecy was well preserved, considering the daily conferences which M. Clemenceau, Mr. Lloyd George, and Signor Orlando had
with their advisers. The fact is that the American commissioners gained practically all their
knowledge of the progress of the work of the
Council from the gossip of the staffs of other
delegations,— as the President, I am informed,
declined to let Sir Maurice Hankey furnish any
of the American Commission with a copy of his
minutes,— or when an American expert or group
of experts was requested by the President to be
present to discuss technical questions. In view
of this ignorance, it would be presumptuous for
me to attempt to comment on the traits of
character exhibited by the heads of states as they
sat in conclave at the President's residence on
the Place des Etats Unis.

That the meetings of the Council of Four were
not entirely harmonious may be stated with substantial certainty. On one occasion soon after

the Council was formed, so it was credibly reported, the President and M. Clemenceau lost their tempers and the session broke up with a considerable exhibition of feeling. This episode was unpleasant, but it was decidedly human. The wonder is that there were not more incidents of the sort, because some of the members of the Council possessed qualities which were by no means patient under the strain of prolonged deliberations.

It is my belief that President Wilson's influence had much to do with preserving peace in the Council of Four. Placid and dignified in manner, he impressed upon others a disposition to be calm in expression and to avoid giving way to emotional impulses. In this particular his influence was undoubtedly superior to that of any other man in the Councils or the Conference, and contributed greatly to the amicable settlements of many vexatious disputes which caused personal irritation and which, but for his considerate and temperate attitude, might have ripened into personal quarrels.

The President's foreign colleagues recognized that he was honestly seeking for firm bases for the future peace of the world. Though they doubtless thought many of his proposals were impracticable and therefore of doubtful value, they respected their author because of his motives, and each of them in his own way endeavored to conform his ideas to those of the President in order to gain his moral support. This was a concession to idealism by the selfish materialism which was so potent in formulating the terms of peace. It bore witness to the general feeling among the delegates to the Conference that Mr. Wilson stood for international morality and justice.

If the President failed in the full realization of his purposes, it was not out of lack of good intentions, but rather because of inexperience in negotiation, of desire to exercise an independent judgment, of exaggeration of the importance of adopting the covenant, and of overconfidence in the motives of others. It was only after the Council of Four had been in session for some time, and after he had committed himself to certain compromises, the justice of which appeared to many to be doubtful, that the President seemed to awake to the fact that he had overestimated the potency of altruism and of abstract justice in the negotiations. From the time that he seemed to come to a realization of the true state of affairs, the statesmen of the Allied Powers found him less pliable and apparently less credulous of their announced intentions. Up to the end, however, he preserved the geniality of manner and the considerate attitude which had from the first marked his intercourse with the leaders at Paris.

It was in the plenary sessions of the Conference on the Preliminaries of Peace that the President's personal gifts showed to the greatest advantage. In the presence of the whole body of delegates his ability as a speaker, his attractive and convincing style of expression, and his dignity of manner made a profound impression on his listeners. He was more at home in addressing a large audience, such as he had at a plenary session, than he was sitting at the council table under the cross-fire of debate. He, of all those who addressed the full assembly of delegates, was listened to with the greatest attention; and his words carried the greatest weight. To the delegations from the smaller countries he was the uncompromising supporter of the ideals which he had declared, the advocate of equal justice for all, the sturdy defender of their rights. In him they placed their confidence and hope.

It is true that, as the terms of peace approached final settlement and as rumors of what the terms were to be spread among the delegates in spite of the secrecy which surrounded them, there grew up in some minds, particularly of those whose national aspirations were reported to be unsatisfied, doubt as to the potential influence which the President had been able to exert over his European colleagues. At first, however, the faith of the delegates in him was unbounded, and he was received by them with enthusiasm, almost with veneration. But after months of waiting in idleness and ignorance of the status of their own national rights, it became noticeable that with the representatives of the smaller nations the President's popularity waned more and more; and though he addressed them with the same excellence of language and proclaimed the same devotion to lofty principles, the reaction upon his hearers was different from what it had been in the earlier sessions, and there was an evident disposition to accept his statements with mental reservations, and not at their face value. In fact, it may be said that the disappointed delegates no longer saw in him a Moses who was to lead the nations to the Promised Land.

Doubtless this change of attitude, which outside the assembly hall of the Conference found expression in whispered criticisms and occasionally in open complaints, was partly due to the President's failure to do all that the grumbling delegates expected of him, expectations which no mortal man could ever have fulfilled because many of the claims founded on national ambitions lapped and overlapped and could never be reconciled so as to satisfy both parties. Thus the President lost favor and prestige through his inability to do the impossible, since with hardly an exception the disappointed delegates blamed him especially for their failure to obtain by the terms of peace tha t which their nations desired. It was one of those unavoidable misfortunes which befall a man who, placed on a pedestal, is idolized as the embodiment of justice by men and by nations whose ideas as to what is just vary, possibly unconsciously, according to their conceptions of what will be of material benefit to themselves.

The President, as we review his career as a peace commissioner at Paris, stands forth as one of the great dominating figures of the Conference, who reached the zenith of his power over the public mind of Europe, over the delegates and over the negotiations at the first plenary session of the Conference. The reasons for his decline in power, a fact which can hardly be questioned, may be one or more of many. First, the loss of his superior position by intimate personal intercourse with the European statesmen, which could have been avoided if he had remained in the United States or if he had declined to sit as a delegate at Paris. Second, his evident lack of experience as a negotiator and his failure to systematize the work of the American Commission and to formulate a programme. Third, his seclusiveness and apparent determination to conduct personally almost every phase of the negotiations and to decide every question alone and independently. Fourth, his willingness to arrange all settlements behind closed doors with the three other heads of states present at the Conference. Fifth, his unavoidable lack of knowledge of the details of some of the simple as well as the intricate problems to be solved. Sixth, his insistence on the adoption of the covenant of the League of Nations, as drafted, and the overcoming of opposition by concessions to national aspirations, the justice of which was at least disputable. Seventh, his loss of the initiative in the formulation of the provisions of the treaties. Eighth, his apparent abandonment of the smaller nations and his tacit denial of the equality of nations by consenting to the creation of an oligarchy of the Great Powers at the Conference and in a modified form in the covenant. And, ninth, the impression, which greatly increased after his return from the United States in March, that the American people were not a unit in support of his aims as to a league of nations, as those aims were disclosed by the report made to the Peace Conference.

This list might be extended, but the reasons stated are sufficient to explain much that occurred at Paris and also many of the features of the treaty of peace with Germany which have been the subject of debate, censure, and denunciation.

It is not to be wondered at, when the proceedings of the Conference are carefully considered, that the Old Tiger of France, with his materialistic motives, his intense patriotism, and his cynical view of transcendental internationalism, became, as he was, the dominant personality in the Peace Conference and the most potent member of the Council of Four. His shrewd and practical methods of negotiation succeeded better than the President's idealism. Yet the latter's personal influence upon the delegates and his success in incorporating in the treaty of peace the covenant of the League of Nations, whatever may be thought of its provisions, entitle him to a place second only to M. Clemenceau among the statesmen who directed affairs at Paris.

The conclusion should not be drawn from the comments which have been made as to the faults in the Treaty of Versailles that the treaty as a whole should be condemned. As a definitive treaty of peace, exclusive of the articles relating to the League of Nations, negotiated in the way and at the time that it was, it would have been difficult to have obtained a better one, considering the numerous conflicting interests and the intemperate spirit of vengeance which then prevailed. The treaty has defects, many defects; it has bad provisions which should not have been included; but the wonder is that, in the circumstances, they are not more general and more glaring.

Wilson

The chief objections raised against the treaty in the United States have been to those articles comprising the covenant of the League of Nations and to those dealing with Shantung. The other settlements, though some are admittedly open to criticism, appear to be generally acceptable.

The interweaving of the League of Nations into various provisions of the treaty, a scheme which raises a question as to the scruples of the author, has, in the opinion of many, tainted the whole document with evil. This is manifestly unjust and evidences a prejudice which results from ignorance or, what is more deplorable, from an unreasonable mental attitude.

The truth is, as some saw it in Paris and as others have seen it since the negotiation and signature of the treaty, there should have been drafted a preliminary treaty of peace, avoiding as far as possible all controversial and complex questions and restoring a state of peace with little delay. When the great need of the world had been thus satisfied, the negotiation of the definitive treaty and the plan for an organization of the nations could have been taken up separately with the care and deliberation to which they

Wilson

were entitled and under conditions more favorable to the formulation of just and wise settlements.

If this course had been adopted, President Wilson would have been spared the vexations and entanglements which surrounded him in Paris and which were in large measure responsible for his failure to hold the first place in the Peace Conference. The drafting of a definitive treaty, including a detailed covenant for the League of Nations, seriously impaired his influence, his prestige, and his reputation. His insistence upon the incorporation of the covenant in the treaty lost him the world leadership which was in his grasp.

III

LLOYD GEORGE

In Mr. Lloyd George, who, in my judgment, was third in prominence and influence among the Big Four, one finds a very different type of man from either of the two who have been considered. While M. Clemenceau and Mr. Wilson entered upon the negotiations with general objects to be attained, the one national and material, the other international and ideal, Mr. Lloyd George, if he had a prepared programme, which I assume he did from my acquaintance with his learned and able advisers, did not follow it persistently. His course was erratic, and he so often shifted his ground that one felt that he had abandoned his plan, or at least that he did not care to follow it rigidly, preferring to depend on his own sagacity to take advantage of a situation. As questions arose, particularly those affected by changing political and military conditions, he decided the British attitude with characteristic quickness of judgment and with a positiveness which impressed one with the alertness rather than the depth of his mind, and with the confidence which

Lloyd George

he felt in his own ability to grasp a subject and decide it in the most expedient way, even though he had not given it the study and thought which other men felt were necessary for a wise decision.

Ready as Mr. Lloyd George was to declare a position on any subject, he seemed to be equally ready to change that position on obtaining further information or on the advice of his expert counselors. He did this with an avowal that he had not previously been in possession of the facts or else with an explanation intended to show that his new attitude was not contradictory of the former one. His explanations were always clever and well presented, but they were not always convincing. The British Premier thus put aside that which had gone before and proceeded to handle the question under discussion as if nothing had occurred to change the course of the debate. Inconsistency never seemed to disturb him or to cause him to hesitate. If he took the trouble to explain a change of attitude, it was out of no sense of obligation to justify himself, but rather in deference to the opinion of others and to prevent complaint. It apparently was a trivial matter to him to change his mind once or twice on a proposed settlement.

Lloyd George

While Mr. Lloyd George was vague as to general principles, which accounted largely for the fluid state of his judgments, he had made certain promises during the parliamentary elections of December, 1918, which he considered binding upon him in the negotiations at Paris. Of these Germany's payment of the costs of the war and the public trial of the Kaiser by an international tribunal of justice attracted the most attention. He was very insistent that the treaty should make these promises good, although he must have known that the first was impossible and the second unwise as well as in defiance of all legal precepts. In addition to his political commitments, he was determined to obtain the cession of the principal German colonies in Africa and the German islands in the Pacific south of the equator, control of Mesopotamia, a protectorate over Egypt, a practical protectorate over Persia in the event that Persian affairs came before the Conference, the destruction of the German naval power and the elimination of the German merchant marine as a rival of Great Britain in the carrying trade of the world. To these well-defined national policies, which were essentially selfish and material, the British Prime

Lloyd George

Minister clung tenaciously and was able to obtain nearly all of them by skillful maneuvering. His idea seemed to be that, if these objects were attained, the decisions as to other matters were of relatively little importance unless British interests were directly affected, and that to study them thoroughly was a needless expenditure of time and energy. It was very evident to any one who was familiar with the subjects that he counted on his skill as a ready debater and on the promptings of his experts to handle the questions satisfactorily when they were presented to the Council of Four or Council of Ten.

Mr. Lloyd George had a pleasing·personality and a hearty manner of address, which won him friends even among those who were disposed to charge him with vacillation. Of him it may be said that he possessed personal magnetism. He was short in stature, and rather thickset. His complexion, which was ruddy and almost as clear as a child's, was set off by an abundance of silvery-white hair brushed back from his broad forehead, and by a short white mustache which curved over his lips. His eyes were keen and twinkling, and when he smiled the wrinkles at the corners were very marked. He would enter

Lloyd George

the council chamber at the Ministry of Foreign
Affairs, generally late, with a quick step, which
on account of its length made it a bit swaggering,
and greet his colleagues with a genial smile and
a bluff heartiness which were attractive.

On taking his seat in the great brocaded armchair between Mr. Balfour and me, he would
usually lean back and ask his secretary in an
audible undertone if there were any notes on the
agenda. If any were handed to him, he would
put on his eyeglasses, examine the papers in a
hasty, offhand way, ask a few questions of the
secretary leaning over the back of his chair, and
then, putting the papers down on the table in
front of him, lean back with his weight on his
right arm and wait composedly the opening of
the session. His manner conveyed the impression
of a man who was satisfied that he had obtained
all the information that he needed to deal with
the several subjects to be discussed by the Council. One could not but admire the complacency
which he showed as to his own ability. In the
conferences of the Council, Mr. Lloyd George
disclosed that his training was that of a parlia-
mentarian rather than that of a diplomat. He
did not speak in the calm, deliberate, and precise

manner in which President Wilson spoke, nor in the analytical and closely reasoned style of Signor Orlando when arguing a point. The British statesman was very much of a rough-and-tumble debater, quick to seize upon the weak points of an opponent and to attack them vigorously, sometimes with sarcasm and ridicule, and often with flat denials of fact. His logic, if one could so call it, was that of an opportunist, and not at all sound or convincing. He was better in attack than in defense, as the latter required detailed knowledge of every phase of the question, while in attacking he could choose his own ground. He did not hesitate to interrupt a speaker with a hasty question or comment, and sometimes, if he seemed to be getting the worse of an argument, he assumed a scoffing and even a blustering manner which did not harmonize with the sedateness of the Council of Ten, though it did seem to fit into the portrait of the famous Welsh politician.

While during a debate he was thus prone to interfere with others, Mr. Lloyd George showed displeasure or annoyance if he was interrupted when speaking or if his statements were challenged. He had held his place in the British

Lloyd George

House of Commons by constant forensic battles. He had used all the arts of a popular political leader to maintain his position, and he had succeeded more by reason of his dynamic personality and by fearlessly defying his enemies than by the superiority of his learning or the strength of his position. All people admire fearlessness and instinctively follow a leader who takes the offensive instead of standing on the defensive. They seem to care far more for this trait than they do for depth of knowledge or soundness of logic. His appreciation of this quality of human nature and his constant exploitation of it in his political career made Lloyd George the Prime Minister of Great Britain. Nothing daunted him. No antagonist was too strongly entrenched to discourage him. His quick wit, his ready tongue, and his self-confidence made him what he was, a great parliamentary leader. In some ways his attainments as a politician were not dissimilar to those of M. Clemenceau, though the latter appeared to be more constant and — to use a vulgar term — less shifty than his British colleague.

In the Councils at Paris these qualities of mind were by no means so effective as in the House of

Lloyd George

Commons or on the political platform. M. Clemenceau sagaciously cast them aside, but Mr. Lloyd George could not. They were his heavy artillery. He would have been lost without them. In the negotiations conducted by the heads of states and foreign ministers of the Five Great Powers, accurate knowledge counted and intellectual ability claimed first place. Without Mr. Balfour's aid and without the constant advice of his subordinates, Mr. Lloyd George would, I fear, have been decidedly outclassed. As it was, his truculence of manner when hard pressed in debate, his attempts to ignore substantial arguments which he was not prepared to answer, and his frequent efforts to enhance the importance of a fact by emphatic declaration were methods that certainly did not carry conviction.

Yet nobody could come into intimate association with Mr. Lloyd George without falling under the spell of his personal charm. One might dislike his methods as those of a politician; one might even feel a measure of contemptuous surprise that he dared to discuss a question of territory without knowing exactly where the territory was; and there might be a feeling of irritation that he changed his mind whenever it

Lloyd George

seemed to him expedient; but with it all one liked the man; it was simply impossible not to like him. His cheeriness, his vivacity, his never-failing good nature, and his delightful humor were assets which counted greatly in his favor.

There was one deplorable phase of the proceedings at Paris for which, I think, Mr. Lloyd George was chiefly though by no means entirely responsible. That was the secrecy which prevailed as to the work of the Council of Ten and later as to that of the Council of Four. Of course a certain measure of secrecy as to individual opinions was necessary while questions were undecided: otherwise there would have been no frankness in the discussions; but to keep decisions hidden even from the delegates of countries whose national rights and interests were affected, until the German treaty was in final form and printed, was certainly contrary to the spirit of open diplomacy and of common justice. Yet this is what actually happened by order of the heads of states.

The creation of the Council of Four was probably due to this desire to shut more tightly the door upon the deliberations of the statesmen who had the last word as to the terms of peace.

Lloyd George

Not that it was the sole reason, but that it was the principal one seems to be the fact. That the idea of splitting the Council of Ten into two bodies originated with Mr. Lloyd George I believe, but do not positively know. The attempt to make President Wilson responsible for it, and to assign as a reason certain attempted actions by the Council of Ten during his brief visit to the United States in February, is absurd, as no action was attempted contrary to his wishes while he was absent. As I have said, my belief is that Mr. Lloyd George was the originator of the plan and probably the author of the announced reason, which was that two councils could cover more ground than a single council, a reason which, though to an extent true, was not the real one.

The British Premier throughout his sojourn in France was in daily touch with the state of affairs in Parliament as well as in Great Britain at large. Never for a moment did he take his hand from the political pulse at home. Though he had been victorious in the December elections, his position was none the less precarious, dependent as it was on a coalition of parties, which is always more or less unstable. Constantly fac-

Lloyd George

ing the possibility of a crisis in his government, Mr. Lloyd George's attitude on various questions arising in the negotiations was undoubtedly affected if not determined by British popular sentiment as it was disclosed from day to day and by the advices which he received from his political lieutenants in London.

While there is a natural disposition to criticize him for his attempts to follow the fluctuations of public opinion rather than to follow a rigid policy, it should be remembered that the tenure of office of a British cabinet is dependent on the will of the House of Commons and that unless a majority supports the Government they are forced to resign. M. Clemenceau and Signor Orlando, though less openly responsive to public opinion than their British colleague and more successful than he in disguising their motives, were nevertheless constrained to consider the wishes of their respective Chambers of Deputies. President Wilson alone was untrammeled by domestic considerations of that nature. He alone was free to act without fear of being deprived of his authority. Unless the three European statesmen watched vigilantly the trend of political opinion in their respective countries, and

trimmed their sails to meet the shifting winds of
that opinion, which in the months following the
armistice were tempestuous and uncertain, any
one of them was liable to be deprived of his
premiership and to be recalled from Paris. This
actually happened later when the Italian Ministry was defeated and Signor Orlando was
superseded in the Peace Conference by Signor
Tittoni as the head of the Italian delegation.

Not only did this watchfulness of public
thought at home affect the points of view of the
European leaders on many of the pending questions, but it induced a desire for secrecy as to the
progress of the negotiations. If the proceedings
were not published, there would not be a constant heckling of the negotiators by their political enemies. At least so they reasoned, although
they ran the risk of acting contrary to an in-
telligent public opinion and of deferring popular
judgment until it was too late to reverse their
action.

It is evident that so far as the Europeans were
concerned, there was a reason for their favoring
secret negotiations; but when they went to the
extent of depriving the delegates from the small
countries — who were vitally interested in the

Lloyd George

terms of peace — of all knowledge of the proceedings of the Councils, they aroused bitter dissatisfaction among those who felt that their national interests and in some cases the sovereign rights of their countries were at stake. It is true that the various delegations were accorded hearings before one or the other of the Councils and permitted to plead their cases, but in the deliberations at which the settlements were decided they were not given an opportunity to participate. If the interests of one of the countries unrepresented on the Councils were in conflict with the interests or the policies of one of the Five Powers, what chance had the small nation to obtain full justice? Then, too, the representatives of Serbia, Rumania, Greece, and others of the lesser states, which had been active belligerents in the war, received practically the same treatment as the unofficial delegations of Armenians, Syrians, and Zionists who appeared before the Council of Ten. Though the former represented independent states and had seats in the Conference, their national rights were determined without their assent by the principal delegates of the Great Powers, who assumed supreme authority and whose determinations were kept secret so far as was possible until the treaty was finally drafted.

There is no doubt that the method adopted was essential to the practical control of the proceedings by the Great Powers, and that it also expedited the negotiations, but in my opinion the sacrifice of the principle of the equality of nations and of the fundamental right of every independent state, the little as well as the large, the weak as well as the powerful, to have a voice in the determination of its own destiny, was too great a price to pay for the advantages gained. The basic principle recognized in international intercourse prior to the war was that before the law all independent nations are equal. That principle has been seriously impaired if not entirely discredited by the proceedings at Paris, and this revival of the old doctrine that even in times of peace the strong shall rule has been so woven into the structure of the League of Nations that it will be a difficult task to resurrect the doctrine of equality and restore it to its place as the first maxim of international law, the fundamental principle of international relations. The hope for such restoration lies in giving first place to legal justice, applied through the medium of international courts, independent of any political or diplomatic international body which may be formed.

It cannot be doubted that President Wilson in agreeing to, if he did not advocate, the primacy of the Great Powers at Paris lost an advantage which he could easily have held had he opposed it. Supported as he was by most if not all of the smaller states represented in the Conference, — at least at the first, since they looked upon him as their firm friend, — he could have maintained his superior position if he had held strictly to the rule of equality and insisted that, if the terms of peace were to be definitive, they should be considered and drafted by general commissions whose reports should be discussed and passed upon in full sessions of the Conference. Even when that normal and customary way was abandoned, he lost another opportunity. Supported as he was by the people of nearly every country, he could have brought tremendous pressure upon his three principal colleagues if he had resisted the policy of extreme secrecy which was followed. He failed to perceive, or else he feared to seize, these chances, and therefore must share the blame with his associates.

Lloyd George

I have stated that Mr. Lloyd George, in my opinion, was principally responsible for the secrecy of the proceedings of the Councils. I know that he showed the greatest perturbation over publicity and most strenuously demanded that the discussions and settlements should be held strictly secret. Though the meetings of the Council of Ten were considered confidential, only an official *communiqué* being given out after a meeting, there frequently appeared in the Parisian press reports of the proceedings which were no doubt embarrassing to the British Government, since they became the subject of interpellation and discussion in Parliament. As nearly all the cases of these unauthorized reports seemed to be in a measure helpful to the French Cabinet in the Chamber of Deputies, it was presumed, not without reason, that the information came from the official group who, independently of the Minister of Foreign Affairs, control in large measure the acts of the Foreign Office in Paris, and who were in constant touch with the proceedings of the Peace Conference.

These published statements greatly annoyed Mr. Lloyd George and caused him to use some very plain and vigorous language about the way news leaked out. He implied rather broadly that since the French Government maintained complete control of the press through its censorship, the publication of this news was for political purposes, and asserted that he, for one, would not stand it. M. Clemenceau listened to these complaints with apparently unruffled temper and replied that he was as desirous as his distinguished confrère to preserve the absolute secrecy of the proceedings, that he deplored the fact that anything had occurred which caused him annoyance, and that he would take steps to prevent further publicity, though he was sure that the source of the information was not the French officials, who were always discreet and honorable.

With M. Clemenceau's assurances Mr. Lloyd George had to be satisfied, at least for the time, but as the French journals, after a brief silence, began again to print inside information concerning the Council, he renewed his complaints. The French Premier expressed deep concern and repeated his assurances that he would do everything that he could to stop the leak. At the same time he pointed out that the London press was publishing reports of the proceedings of the Council which were very disturbing to him and his Government and invited the attacks of his enemies in the Chamber of Deputies. Mr. Lloyd George blustered about this insinuation that his people were doing the very thing of which he complained, and declared that this improper publicity was the result of having so many persons present at the sessions of the Council, and that the only way to check it was to reduce the number. In truth, M. Clemenceau and Mr. Lloyd George were equally desirous for political reasons to have certain matters made public, but each of them wished to decide what those matters should be.

The result of these conditions was the organization of the Council of the Heads of States. There is no question but that the new method of conducting business was in the main effective as to secrecy. Only the most fragmentary information came through the closed doors of the President's residence, where the Big Four sat in conclave. Not only the public, but the delegates to the Conference as well, remained in ignorance of the proceedings. Though the general discontent increased, and the mutterings — particularly of the representatives of the press assembled in Paris — grew louder and more bitter against

this policy of silence and mystery, Mr. Lloyd
George did not appear to be disturbed. On the
contrary, he was even more insistent that the
seal of secrecy should remain unbroken.

The climax of this dislike — or possibly I
should say, this fear — of publicity on the part of
the British statesman came at a meeting of the
Council of Ten held at the President's house
about the middle of April, which, according to
the notice, was summoned to consider the publicity to be given to the terms of peace before
the treaty was delivered to the Germans, but
which was, in fact, summoned to devise means
to prevent the terms from becoming public.
The meeting was one of the most extraordinary
ever held in connection with a great international
congress, most extraordinary as to subject, discussion, and result.

I do not feel that I can give a detailed account
of what occurred at this meeting, but it may be
said that Mr. Lloyd George held the opinion —
an opinion which he freely expressed outside the
Council — that in order to keep secret the terms
of the treaty as long as possible the delegates of
the lesser co-belligerent states, who had been
excluded from all participation in the drafting of

the document, ought not even to see the full text before the Germans saw it, and that all delegates, friends and foes alike, should simply be directed to "sign here." This opinion — which was evidently based on the assumed right of the Great Powers to dictate to the Conference — was apparently made with the idea that it would be too late to propose changes in the treaty after the terms had been imposed on the Germans, and that the terms could not become the subject of political attack or public criticism at home while the Germans were considering them and formulating objections to them.

The result of the meeting was a decree or order by the Council of Four that a summary, and not the text, of the treaty should be laid before the delegates on the afternoon preceding the delivery of the document to the German representatives, and that no delegate should be permitted to debate the terms unless it was in a perfunctory manner, and in no event to attempt to amend them. The conduct of the proceedings being in the hands of M. Clemenceau, the programme was certain to go through. Altogether this was the most amazing and most indefensible exhibition of the despotism of the Five Powers that

Lloyd George

was given at the Conference. It was in utter disregard of the legal rights of sovereignty in times of peace, a reversion to physical might as the measure of authority. The impression made upon the delegates of the smaller nations can be imagined. They were aghast at such treatment, as well they might be, but without an influential leader what could they do? Some of them said frankly that they expected nothing less of M. Clemenceau and Mr. Lloyd George, but that they had confidently believed that President Wilson would not permit such unjust treatment, that they were in despair at his desertion of them, and that they were convinced that he was not the strong man they had thought him, since he had surrendered to those who favored the primacy of the Five Great Powers. Mr. Wilson from that time forward lost the commanding position which he had held with the lesser nations. They no longer had confidence in his courage and influence.

The fact is that the two leading European statesmen were secretive through fear of the effect of publicity on their political fortunes, and the President was secretive by nature. As for Signor Orlando, he belonged to that school of statesmanship of which a cardinal principle is and always had been secretiveness as to discussions, agreements, and alliances, national and international. His training and experience in government made his approval certain. With the Japanese, secretiveness is a racial characteristic.

Yet, in my opinion, Mr. Lloyd George went further than any of his colleagues would have gone in advocating the suppression of information, and he urged it with a frankness which showed an utter lack of regard for, or possibly lack of appreciation of, the attributes of sovereignty. Had there been a trained legal mind among the Big Four, other than that of Signor Orlando, it might have been different. Unfortunately, the three principal statesmen of that powerful group were without such training, although both Mr. Wilson and Mr. Lloyd George had begun life as members of the legal profession. They were unable to think in terms of international law or to model their procedure to conform to the custom and usage of nations. The rights and liberties of independent states were in peril. They needed a jealous guardian to protect them from invasion. There was none.

Lloyd George '

It was a serious defect in the constitution of the Council, which was reflected in other phases of its proceedings.

The insistence of the British Prime Minister on secrecy at Paris was one of the manifestations of that opportunism which has distinguished his public career. Expediency controlled in a marked degree his actions during the negotiations as it had done his policies and acts as leader of the Government in Parliament. He did not accept a principle, or at least showed no disposition to apply it, unless it appeared to lead to some practical advantage to his Government, and if he found that his anticipation as to the result was wrong, he unhesitatingly abandoned the principle and assumed another.

When one reviews the unusual political career of Mr. Lloyd George, and sees how successfully he managed to hold his own with the conservative element of the British people and to placate the radicals — even those of the more advanced type—by meeting them part way or by appearing to acquiesce in their extreme views, his shrewdness and sagacity in the management of contending political factions arouse admiration for his ability, though it does not follow that they

Lloyd George

excite the same emotion as to his devotion to principle or to his constancy of purpose.

More than once, while the negotiations were in progress at Paris, Mr. Lloyd George returned to London and appeared in the House of Commons for the purpose of leading the Government in repelling an attack by the Opposition. On those occasions he so adroitly explained the Government's policies and so brilliantly pictured the satisfactory progress of the work of the Peace Conference that the attempted criticisms which followed were feeble and futile. Aggressive, sanguine, and cheerfully willing to face his opponents, he successfully combated their criticisms. Having routed his antagonists at home, he returned to Paris unquestionably stronger in his own eyes, as well as in the eyes of others, because of his evident mastery of the parliamentary situation.

While opinions may differ as to whether Mr. Lloyd George is a great statesman, no one can truthfully deny that he is a great politician who shows a remarkable insight into human nature and a skill in the manipulation of political forces which have enabled him to hold his place in the most difficult circumstances. Through the critical periods of the war he maintained his ascendancy by his ability to play off faction against faction, and by his agility in keeping his equilibrium on a very flimsy structure built up of discordant and even of hostile elements. Often his position was extremely precarious, but his wit and readiness as a speaker always saved him from defeat in the House of Commons.

While he brought this cleverness to his aid in the negotiations at Paris, sudden changes of position and the endeavor to divide his opponents by encouraging first one and then another were methods unsuited to the settlement of international differences. They did not work in the same way that they did in the sphere of domestic politics. His methods carried the impression, possibly an erroneous one, that he was unreliable, in fact, wabbly. This feeling decidedly impaired his influence in the Councils, as it did among the delegates in general. Though his keenness of mind was fully appreciated, the way in which it was used aroused doubt as to his sincerity, and nothing can be more detrimental to a negotiator than to be credited with insincerity. The consequence was that every position taken and every suggestion offered by the British leader was suspected and a hidden purpose was frequently presumed when doubtless there was none.

But Mr. Lloyd George, always looking at a question from the point of view of expediency, would have been seriously handicapped in the council chamber had he not relied on the experience and knowledge of Mr. Balfour, Lord Milner, and Sir Eyre Crowe, who foresaw whither the expedient might lead him. He accepted the judgment of others unless their judgment came in direct conflict with his political programme for the day, and even then he was willing to modify his views to meet, at least partially, the course which they advised.

Mr. Lloyd George possessed a wonderfully alert mind which fairly bubbled over with restless energy. He made decisions rapidly and with little regard for details or fundamental principles. If he fell into error through incomplete knowledge or wrong deductions, he picked himself up with a laugh or a witticism and went ahead as if nothing had happened. In debate he was vigorous and often impetuous. If it were shown that his argument was based on false premises, he unblushingly changed his premises, but not his argument. The audacity with which he ignored logic was a subject of frequent com-. ment. He, in my opinion, had the quickest mind of the Big Four, but it seemed to lack stability. He gave the impression of a man who through force of circumstances had been compelled to jump at conclusions instead of reaching them through the surer but slower processes of reason. By many he was credited with superficial knowledge and careless judgment. This opinion was a natural result of the way in which he pressed forward, showing impatience that others were not willing to render decisions on evidence which he deemed entirely sufficient, but which his colleagues considered questionable.

Vivacious, good-tempered, and possessing a strong sense of humor, Mr. Lloyd George was socially an attractive person, while in debate his cleverness in finding the weak spots in an opponent's armor and his utter indifference to his own errors made him a dangerous antagonist. He attacked with vigor and he defended by attacking. But this unusual man possessed none of the arts of diplomacy. He was not by nature a negotiator. His successes at Paris — and they were not a few — were largely due to the excellent advice which was given him, and which he wisely received.

IV

ORLANDO

Signor Orlando possessed physical and mental characteristics which have left pleasant memories of intercourse with him. Short and rotund in person, with thick white hair worn pompadour and a white mustache partially covering his rather full lips, he was not in personal appearance typical of Italy. His shortness of stature, which was about that of Mr. Lloyd George, was emphasized by his usual custom of wearing a close-fitting sack coat, which he generally kept tightly buttoned. With a friendly eye and a smile which dimpled his cheeks, one knew at a glance that he was of a kindly nature and not disposed to quarrel without a sufficient provocation. His clear complexion and unwrinkled face indicated good health and a capacity to enjoy life.

The mentality of Signor Orlando was moulded on different lines from those of any other member of the Council of the Heads of States. It had been trained and developed in the field of jurisprudence, and possessed the precision of thought

Harris & Ewing, Washington, D.C.

and clearness of expression which are the attributes of a mind accustomed to the exactness of legal expressions. In some ways it was harder to judge accurately the mental qualities of the Italian statesman than those of his confrères because his inability to speak or to understand English debarred him in a measure from the informal discussions of the Council, which were generally conducted in that language out of consideration for President Wilson and Mr. Lloyd George. With the aid of Professor Mantoux, however, he was able to participate more than might have seemed possible in the circumstances.

It is fitting to digress for a moment and to say a word of Professor Mantoux, who wore a French captain's uniform, and was inherited by the Council of Ten from the Supreme War Council. No interpreter could have performed his onerous task with greater skill than he. Possessing an unusual memory for thought and phrase, he did not interpret sentence by sentence, but, while an address or statement was being made, he listened intently, occasionally jotting down a note with the stub of a lead pencil. When the speaker had finished, this remarkable linguist would translate his remarks into English or into French as the case might be, without the least hesitation and with a fluency and completeness which were almost uncanny. Even if the speaker had consumed ten, fifteen, or twenty minutes, the address was accurately repeated in the other language, while Professor Mantoux would employ inflection and emphasis with an oratorical skill that added greatly to the perfectness of the interpretation. No statement was too dry to make him inattentive or too technical for his vocabulary. Eloquence, careful reasoning, and unusual style in expression were apparently easily rendered into idiomatic English from the French, or *vice versa*. He seemed almost to take over the character of the individual whose words he translated, and to reproduce his emotions as well as his thoughts. His extraordinary attainments were recognized by every one who benefited by them, and his services commanded general admiration and praise.

In addition to the information obtained through the excellent interpretations of Professor Mantoux, Signor Orlando had the aid of Baron Sonnino, the Italian Minister of Foreign Affairs, who spoke English without an accent and understood it perfectly. The Baron, white-haired and white-mustached, with a florid complexion and a genial smile, which was a bit saturnine, belonged to the diplomats of the old school, and was disposed to practice their methods. Practical and deliberate in urging his views, which were little affected by idealistic considerations, he sought always to secure material benefits for his country. It was clearly national interest rather than abstract justice which controlled his mind. In appearance at least he impressed one as superior to his leader. Possibly he was; but then, the same might have been said of Mr. Balfour, who, in addition to his dignity of appearance, was recognized to be the intellectual superior of Mr. Lloyd George. This latter superiority could not, however, be attributed to Baron Sonnino. Signor Orlando was intellectually as well equipped as he.

The Italian Premier possessed certain qualities of mind which were of an exceptional order and which marked him as a statesman rather than a politician. In fact, his political instinct seemed to be deficient, and events proved him by no means skillful as a political leader. As an opportunist he was a failure. But when we analyze his statesmanlike qualities, which were clearly in evidence at Paris, I think that it is not going too far to say that no member of the Council of Four, or of the Council of Ten for that matter, was his superior in presenting a clear, concise, and comprehensive argument during the course of an extemporaneous debate.

Signor Orlando's mind seemed to work automatically in analyzing, classifying, and arranging the points in a controversy. Having stored away each essential fact or reason in the proper compartment of his brain, he called it forth at just the right place in his argument and impressed it with just the right value. He did not exaggerate the importance of a fact or ignore the strength of an adverse argument. When he had finished debating a question, one had to admit, whether he agreed with him or not, that he had made as logical a presentation of his side of the case as it was possible to make, and that there was nothing to add. As for the effectiveness of Signor Orlando's arguments, that is another matter, in view of the preconceived ideas and natural bias of his listeners, but no one heard him without realizing his strength as an advocate. The fact is, however, that the way to succeed in the Council was to offer some form of compromise which

Orlando

would harmonize conflicting positions. When he attempted this, he showed to less advantage.

I believe that the excellent character of the arguments made by Signor Orlando was in a measure due to his experience as a jurist and to the analytical method of thinking which he had acquired. His colleagues in the Council of Four were not so well equipped as he for discussing a legal question or preparing a legal formula. This is an important attainment in a negotiator when one considers that a treaty is essentially a law and that its preparation requires technical legal knowledge and experience. As was too often manifest, the value of logic and evidence was not so fully appreciated by M. Clemenceau, President Wilson, and Mr. Lloyd George as it was by the learned Italian jurisconsult. With him no time was wasted on side issues or in announcing generalities which sounded well, but could not be concretely applied. In speaking he did not grope about for something to say. He knew where lay the strength and where the weakness of his case. He pressed the former with vigor and assurance, and he defended the latter with skill.

Occasionally in the heat of debate, especially if interrupted by M. Clemenceau with some

Orlando

caustic comment, as happened more than once, Signor Orlando's Latin temper would flame. His eyes would flash; his voice would rise as if surcharged with emotion; his hands would add emphasis to his words; and his sentences would pour forth like a torrent. Yet, even under the spur of indignation or anger, the logical trend of his argument was never interrupted or diverted. His intellect functioned normally, however strongly he was stirred by his emotions. And the Old Tiger, whose ferocity of manner was, I am sure, often assumed from the mere love of baiting an opponent, would lean back in his chair with half-closed eyes and immobile countenance, watching the effect of his words, doubtless hoping that he had disconcerted the speaker. If he did cherish that hope in the case of his Italian colleague, he cherished it in vain.

Signor Orlando enjoyed a joke and relished a good story, particularly if it was illustrative of a matter under discussion or was concerning some well-known character, living or dead. He was always jovial and seemingly in a good humor. When an afternoon session of the Council of Ten was ended, and the attendants brought a large tea-table into the chamber from an adjoining room, he always remained to gossip and enjoy the society of the men who had been present. But during the discussion of a question in the Council, Signor Orlando never interlarded his remarks with anecdotes and witty sayings, evidently considering that to do so would weaken his argument and would be out of harmony with the dignity of so serious a business as that in hand.

In my opinion the Italian statesman was entirely right in not imitating the seeming flippancy of some of his colleagues, who appeared to think that an informal and jocular manner was an actual aid in the settlement of a question which might involve the sovereignty over an extensive territory or even the life of a nation. Under certain conditions a humorous remark, if tactfully introduced, may avoid a quarrel or prevent a regrettable incident in a discussion which has reached a point where tempers are aroused and near the explosive point; but the constant interjection of witticisms, though they may be received with smiles and laughter, detracts materially from the influence of the one who utters them.

My impression is — though it is only an im-

pression — that Signor Orlando came to Paris
with the definite purpose of obtaining, so far as
the Adriatic was concerned, the territorial concessions laid down in the Pact of London, and
that the inclusion of the city of Fiume in the
Italian claims was originally advanced for the
purpose of bargaining with the Jugo-Slavs, who
were putting forward excessive claims for por-
tions of the territory conceded to Italy by the
London Agreement. But the reason for the
inclusion of Fiume in the Italian demands is of
little importance compared with the reason for
the subsequent insistence with which the demand
was pressed. Introduced as something with
which to barter in the event that the Italian
claims along the Dalmatian coast were curtailed
in the interest of the Jugo-Slavs, an argument in
favor of annexation to Italy was built up on the
principle of self-determination, that phrase which
has aroused so many false hopes and caused so
much despair since it was coined, and which is a
continuing source of discontent and turmoil in
the world. He especially emphasized the prepon-
derance of Italians in the population of Fiume
because he was led to believe that the President
would support this principle.

Orlando

Signor Orlando, soon after his arrival in Paris, found the situation such that he came to the conclusion that if he remained firm in his claim for the port he would succeed in obtaining it for Italy. This course naturally appealed to him, since success would strengthen his political position at Rome, which was endangered by the probability that the full grant under the Pact of London could not be attained. Thus the claim was converted from one put forward to surrender in a compromise, if I am correct in my surmise, to one which it was possible to secure.

Convinced of the substantial certainty that the President would in the end consent to the cession, and feeling assured that the British and French would not object, a propaganda in favor of Fiume for Italy was begun at Rome, so that when the annexation actually took place the Italian people would acclaim Signor Orlando and his statesmanship, and he would reap the full political benefit of the achievement. Possibly, too, it was thought that a strong manifestation of national feeling would make certain the President's favorable decision.

The trouble was that the policy adopted was based on a false belief as to the President's

ultimate agreement that the city should come
under Italian sovereignty. When Signor Orlando
and Baron Sonnino awoke to the fact that they
had been misled, and that the President was
adamant in refusing to admit Italy's claim to
Fiume in spite of the rule as to self-determination, they were in a sad predicament. They had
started a fire of sentiment among the Italian
people which had spread beyond their control.
They had no alternative but to continue to
struggle for Italian control over the little city,
hoping that they might through some compromise succeed in obtaining what all Italy was
clamoring for, because failure meant the overthrow of the Orlando Ministry. One can imagine
the feelings of the Italian delegation toward
those who had encouraged them to assume a
position from which there had been left no way
to retreat.

The negotiations had continued through confidential channels and in the Council of Four
until the time approached when the Germans
were to receive the treaty of peace. As a last
resort Signor Orlando let it be understood that,
unless the Council conceded Italy's right to
Fiume, the Italian delegation had no other course

than to withdraw from the Conference. It was, I think, a threat made in desperation and was never intended to be carried out. It, however, had the opposite effect on Mr. Wilson from that which was intended. It aroused his ire and made him stubborn. He determined to meet it in a way which was most unusual.

On the evening of April 23d the President issued a public statement on Fiume and Italy's unjustifiable claim to the city, which was in fact if not in purpose an appeal to the Italian people over the head of their Government. The statement was temperate, well-balanced, and logically sound, but, issued at a time when feeling in Italy was at fever heat, it caused a tremendous sensation. Doubtless President Wilson, remembering the unparalleled enthusiasm of his reception in Italy when he visited that country in January, believed that his popularity was sufficient to change the tide of public sentiment and that the Italian people would perceive the injustice of the claim to Fiume because he declared that it was unjust. The storm of abuse and insult with which the statement was received from one end of Italy to the other must have opened the President's eyes to the fact, which had not been

hidden from others, that his popularity with the
peoples of Europe was rapidly receding, and that
they were no longer willing to accept his declarations as the utterances of the inspired leader
of international thought, the apostle of a new
gospel.

Signor Orlando was very angry at this attempt
to rouse Italian public opinion against his Fiume
policy, for so he interpreted Mr. Wilson's statement. He issued a counter-statement, and on
the 24th departed from Paris for Rome, as did
Baron Sonnino. However, the Italian statesmen,
after their anger had cooled, and after they had
had time to consider the possible consequences
upon Italian interests of their continued absence
from the Conference, swallowed their pride and
returned to Paris. Convinced that Italy was
solidly behind him, and that the President had
failed in his appeal and was no longer in favor
with the Italian people, Signor Orlando resumed
his seat in the Council, giving no evidence that
anything had happened to mar the cordial
relations which existed between him and his
associates.

This incident showed the volatile temperament of the Italian Premier more clearly than

anything else that occurred at Paris. Possessed of the emotional intensity of his race, the sudden and extraordinary action of the President, which he construed as a personal affront, made him furious, as it might have done a man of a more phlegmatic nature. On the impulse of the moment, he left Paris, intending undoubtedly not to return. Then, as his rage subsided under the soothing influence of popular approval, and as he reviewed more calmly the situation, he decided that it would be impolitic to remain away from the council table where the terms of peace with Austria were to be drafted or to be absent when the treaty was delivered to the German plenipotentiaries. It is said that added pressure was exerted on the Italians by a threat to abandon entirely the terms of the Pact of London unless they returned immediately to Paris. I have no doubt, however, that Signor Orlando inwardly burned with indignation at the President and at those who had, during the early days of the negotiation, encouraged the belief that the President would assent to the cession of Fiume.

All the clandestine interviews and intrigues had come to naught; and when the Italian delegates returned to Paris, they were not resumed.

Orlando

Signor Orlando and Baron Sonnino were too sagacious to pursue again a course which had ended so disastrously. As an eminent Italian diplomat, one of the Premier's close friends, said to me: "We know now that we dealt from the first with the wrong people. They held out false hopes. They did not tell us the truth. We relied on their advice, and now see where we are! We won't make that mistake again."

However, the damage had been done and could not be undone. The public mind in Italy had been so inflamed that nothing but Italian control of Fiume would satisfy the nation. With that practically impossible, in view of the uncompromising attitude of the President, the overthrow of the Orlando Government was only a question of time unless something unforeseen occurred to affect the situation. But by neither word nor manner did Signor Orlando show his feelings. Even up to the time when the defeat of his Government was certain to take place within a few days, and it was substantially settled that Signor Tittoni would succeed him at Paris as the head of the Italian delegation, the cheerfulness and good humor of the retiring Premier never forsook him. He accepted his approaching political overthrow with a fine spirit. In these trying circumstances he was the same pleasant, smiling gentleman that he had been during the early sessions of the Council of Ten.

Just how far Signor Orlando was influenced in his policy as to Fiume by Baron Sonnino, I do not know. There were many competent observers who were disposed to lay the responsibility for it on the latter's shoulders, as he was a past-master in arranging settlements through secret agreements. No one in the Council of Ten was so adept as he in negotiations of that sort. Persuasive and plausible, with a manner that impressed his listener with the sense of being the specially favored recipient of important information, Baron Sonnino was unquestionably successful in winning to his support those who were susceptible to this species of flattery, and who had a generous opinion of their own importance. Where the Baron failed was in his overvaluation of the support which he won in this way. Had that not been the case, the Italian plan in regard to the Adriatic would have been successful and the Orlando Government, of which Baron Sonnino was so influential a member, would have been stronger than ever at Rome.

Orlando

What has been said of Baron Sonnino is not by way of criticism of him as a man, but of the school of diplomacy to which he belonged. The pity is that all the intrigues and secretiveness, from which the Peace Conference suffered so grievously, did not end as the Fiume affair ended. If the Conference had done nothing else than discredit diplomacy of that sort, it would have been well worth while. Unfortunately, others who practiced similar methods were able to form combinations and make bargains to the mutual and material advantage of their countries. Baron Sonnino's reputation as a clever diplomat and negotiator who was credited — I think unjustly — with hiding his real objects did not help him, while other statesmen, less known in diplomacy and possibly less frank in purpose, engaged in the same practices that he did with impunity and with frequent success.

The fact is, when one who knows what went on in Paris outside the recorded proceedings considers the months during which the Conference was in session, he cannot deny that there was a lot of hypocrisy practiced, a lot of pretense about doing things openly and stating things candidly when secrecy and intrigue were only too evident.

Orlando

One might not like Baron Sonnino's policies and might feel that they flouted the conscience of the nations and were out of harmony with the spirit of the times, but no one could charge him with being a hypocrite. He was in fact far less blameworthy than some who criticized him. Whatever may have been thought of the Italian Minister of Foreign Affairs by these self-righteous negotiators, he was a more reliable man than they, a better man with whom to deal. He was without question an able diplomat, possessing poise and sagacity, while as a companion he was all that could be desired.

Neither Signor Orlando nor Baron Sonnino took as active a part in the debates on general questions which came before the Council of Ten as did the representatives of the United States, France, and Great Britain. Signor Orlando was always ready to give his opinion on such subjects when asked, and he did it with the clearness of statement and logical presentation of reasons of which he was master. When, however, the question was one which had to do with the national interests of Italy, he appeared to be eager to express his views, and seized the first opportunity to address the Council. It was also

Orlando

observable that in any discussion which touched his government or people even so remotely as the establishment of a precedent or policy which might be later invoked against them, Signor Orlando spoke with greater earnestness and much more emphatically than he did on other occasions.

This was evidence of a fact, already mentioned, that the Italian statesmen concentrated their entire effort on the advancement of the material welfare of their country. It is impossible to deny that Italy, however favorably or sympathetically her course may be viewed, entered the war on conditions which in the event of victory by the Allies ensured her future territorial and economic expansion. She sought a good bargain, and Great Britain and France, in view of the conditions existing in April, 1915, were forced to accede to her terms. That same dominant purpose was apparent throughout the negotiations at Paris. Having secured to a large extent the rewards promised a month before Italy declared war against Austria-Hungary, which were embodied in the Pact of London, the Italian representatives at the Peace Conference sought further advantages by advancing new claims. Of course these claims were selfish and not based primarily on international justice, but in that they did not differ from the claims of other Allied Governments. The difference lay, as I see it, in the fact that the Italians urged their claims frankly and without subterfuge, while others, seeking to hide their nationalistic purposes, demanded that their claims should be recognized on the ground that to do so would make for the future peace of the world and for the welfare of the inhabitants of the territories the possession of which they coveted.

While Signor Orlando had taken part in secret negotiations as to Fiume and had endeavored to obtain his object by bringing personal influence to bear on others, it always seemed to me that the secretive method employed contradicted the frankness and openness which he otherwise displayed. He was certainly not by nature disposed to deceive as to his purpose. Possibly he, and Baron Sonnino as well, was too frank, from the point of view of expediency. In any event, apparent frankness, seasoned by assertions of high moral purpose and garnished with unctuous precepts and platitudes, succeeded where real frankness failed. To admit openly that one was impelled by selfish motives was an offense to those who proclaimed their own altruism, whatever their true motives might have been. It was not playing the game according to the rules. The truth is there was at Paris too much lip virtue and too little heart virtue in the settlements that were reached.

The Italian aspirations conflicted more with those of France than with those of any other of the Great Powers. In the Balkans, and to an extent in Asia Minor, they came into direct conflict in the endeavor of each country to extend its sphere of commercial influence in those regions. It was when these questions were being considered that M. Clemenceau and Signor Orlando crossed swords in debate. While I think that The Tiger's domineering manner and sarcastic comments had a subduing effect on the Italian, he replied with vigor and defended his position with skillful parry and counter-thrust, in spite of the interruptions of the older statesman, who was or pretended to be very much out of temper.

As a rule the impression made by the debate was that for logic and force of reasoning Signor Orlando had the better of the argument. He

Orlando

seemed to know his case more thoroughly and to present it more convincingly than did his French adversary. In fact, if the latter had not been the great personality that he was, he would often have been forced to acknowledge defeat. But he never did. Clemenceau defeated was unthinkable to Clemenceau, and that attitude had unquestionably a potent influence on his associates. As a consequence Signor Orlando did not triumph as frequently as he otherwise might have done in his word combats with the fierce old champion of France, who treated him — I believe intentionally — with far less consideration than he did Mr. Wilson and Mr. Lloyd George.

Though Signor Orlando possessed admirable traits of character and exhibited a skill in debate which none of his confrères excelled, he was nevertheless the least influential of the Big Four and had the least to do with formulating the terms of peace with Germany. This was doubtless due in large measure to the relative military, naval, and financial strength of the Great Powers represented in the Council of Four. Comparison by this standard — which, it is to be regretted, was the principal standard in weighing influence at the Peace Conference — tended to place

Orlando

Italy in the background and to subordinate the views of her statesmen. I know also that some felt that the Italian Government had driven too sharp a bargain with the Entente in 1915, and was now demanding more than its pound of flesh, in spite of the small part, which the more critical in Europe asserted, Italy had taken in the later months of the struggle. There seemed to be a disposition to repudiate the Italian claims or at least to reject many of them. It was with evident reluctance that France and Great Britain conceded their treaty obligations. Neither of them vigorously supported Italy when her claims were urged. The attitude seemed to be that of tolerance for a nation which had not won by arms a right to a voice in the decisions, but was by agreement entitled to it. It was therefore especially fortunate for the Italian people that they had in Signor Orlando so well-trained a statesman, so talented an advocate, and so keen a logician to represent them at the Conference. He could not be and was not ignored. Another representative less able might have been.

A review of the foregoing estimate of the personalities of the four statesmen composing

Orlando

the Council of the Heads of States, in whose hands, it may be said, rested the political and economic future of the world, shows that they each possessed qualities of mind which fitted them to be leaders of men, but which did not necessarily equip them to act as negotiators. I think candor compels one to admit, however much he may admire the superior attainments of the Big Four, that it was a misfortune for the nations that the actual formulation of the treaty with Germany was assumed by them.

In the first place, the only one of them who had the legal or diplomatic experience necessary for such a task was Signor Orlando, the least influential of the Council, and the one who was handicapped by not knowing English, in which language the proceedings were chiefly conducted. Of the others, President Wilson thought like a professor advocating a pet theory and expanded his philosophic ideas in a series of epigrams, which sounded well, but which were difficult of practical application, if not of definition. Mr. Lloyd George, who lacked the background which only a thorough student of history could have, was an opportunist, who jumped to conclusions without going through the reasoning processes which are necessary for wise statesmanship. Careless in thought, he was equally careless in speech. Accuracy of expression, so essential in the final settlement of an international question, was not one of his attainments. M. Clemenceau never bothered himself with the actual wording of a decision. The general principle was all that interested him. The technical phraseology he left to the Secretariat General, directing them to send the decisions of the Council of Ten to the drafting committee. A more unsystematic and loose way of conducting business of such moment can hardly be imagined. To term it inexpert is a mild characterization.

To other delegates, appreciative from previous experience of the importance of exact and definite expression, this lax and haphazard procedure caused grave concern, though it did not seem to disturb any members of the Council of Four. Fortunately, the drafting committee included such trained international jurists as Dr. James Brown Scott, for the United States; Mr. — now Sir — Cecil J. B. Hurst, of the British Foreign Office; and M. Henri Fromagéot, of the French Ministry of Foreign Affairs. To their legal knowledge, carefulness, and industry are due the phraseology of the majority of the articles of the treaty and their orderly arrangement. One dreads to think what the document would have looked like if it had not passed through their experienced hands.

If I were asked to state the strongest motives influencing the conduct of each member of the Council of Four during the Peace Conference, I would state them as follows: M. Clemenceau — protection of France from future German attack, indemnification for her war losses, and the perpetuation of her international power in the world; President Wilson — the creation of a league of nations to make permanent the terms of peace, to prevent war, and to supervise international relations in the future; Mr. Lloyd George — the satisfaction of British public opinion, measured in terms of political success and commercial advantage; and Signor Orlando — the expansion of Italy's territorial sovereignty and economic power.

Of these controlling motives that of President Wilson was on a higher ethical plane than that of any of his colleagues. He unquestionably felt that a great moral duty rested on the victorious nations to make great wars impossible for

the future. He believed that this could be done
by organizing the peoples of the world into a
league of nations. It was an idea which appealed
to his intellectual conception that he was devoted
to the welfare of mankind, and to his firm conviction that he was destined to be the leader of the
nations, the commanding figure in this feder-
ation of the world. The theory of the proposed
organization was an appealing one. There was
little that could be urged against the general
principle of union for the sake of peace. It was
in the application of the principle and in attempting to make the theory workable in practice that
the difficulty lay. The President should have
realized — possibly he did — that unless the
Great Powers subordinated their selfish and
materialistic interests to the altruistic purposes
which impelled him to concentrate his efforts
on the drafting and adoption of the covenant,
their support of the League would be merely the
expression of a moral sentiment, provided it did
not constitute a practical agency to protect them
in settlements which satisfied their selfish desires.

Consider and answer these questions, which
are significant as to the spirit which prevailed
among the Great Powers: Why did the French

Orlando

statesmen hesitate to accept the covenant until an added guaranty against German aggression had been substantially agreed upon with President Wilson and Mr. Lloyd George? Why did Italy threaten to withdraw from the Conference and not to become a member of the League until a favorable settlement as to Fiume had been reached, even though it had nothing to do with the treaty with Germany? Why did the Japanese let it be known that they would not join the League unless the German rights in Shantung were ceded to their empire?

The manifest answers to these questions show that selfish motives were superior to moral obligations with the European Powers and with Japan. The attitude seems to have been: Give us all that we demand and we will aid in building a wall for the protection of that which we have obtained.

These incidents, with others which might be cited, are manifestations of the weak influence that abstract justice and the desire for the common good exerted on the Great Powers, and of the impracticability of relying unreservedly on their support of joint action, through an international organization, which was in any way detrimental to their material interests. From the theoretical standpoint of the moral philosopher, good faith and a sense of justice are irresistible forces in the relations between nations, but practically — and we must look to the practical in the world of the present — selfishness is, and I fear will continue to be, the supreme impulse of nations in their dealings with one another, until mankind is morally regenerated.

If the treaty of peace with Germany is critically analyzed in order to determine the motives which found expression in the settlements contained in its hundreds of articles, I do not think the brief statement of these motives which I have made will appear to be prejudiced or unjust. From the treaty terms there is much that can be learned of the psychology of the statesmen who were most influential in formulating them. Such a study, if it is made carefully and impartially, will, I believe, supplement and confirm this review of the characters, the aims, the successes and the failures of the Big Four of the Peace Conference at Paris. In later years, when the results of their labors find actual expression, historians may render a different verdict as to these men, but from the viewpoint of the present

Orlando

I can reach no other than that which it has been my endeavor to state without favor and with entire candor.

The negotiations at Paris may be described as a conflict between altruism and selfishness, between the ideal and the material, between the theoretical and the practical, between principle and expediency; a conflict in which President Wilson, representing the higher standards, was outmaneuvered by the forces of self-interest and opportunism. The consequence was a treaty in which national rather than international interests are emphasized, and through which are scattered seeds of dissatisfaction and discord. No one imbued with the longing for a peace founded on justice can study the treaty of peace with Germany without a keen sense of disappointment as to certain of the terms of settlement or without a feeling of apprehension as to the future. The treaty restored a legal state of peace among the nations; in that was its virtue, for it responded to the supreme longing and need of the world. As for the League of Nations, which is to be an instrument of performance as well as the guardian of this great international compact, it is charged with giving permanency to settlements which, in view of the nature of some of them, invite modification or annulment. Unless these defects are remedied, unless the principle of the equality of nations is recognized, and unless legal justice is emphasized, the Peace of Versailles will be in many of its provisions temporary and not permanent.

IMPRESSIONS OF OTHER STATESMEN

at the Peace Conference

IMPRESSIONS

A MAN who has taken a prominent part in public affairs is naturally subjected to critical observation by those who come in contact with him. There exists a popular belief, gained from various sources, as to his character and attainments, which one is curious to test by personal acquaintance. What is it that has given this man a reputation for greatness, for shrewdness, for wisdom? Wherein lie his powers of leadership? Has he the traits and qualities with which he is credited? Does he possess weaknesses, of which the man in the street knows nothing? Is the popular judgment concerning him accurate? What is his real personality?

It is with such questions that one approaches a leader in the world of thought or action. Almost invariably on first acquaintance an impression is formed of the man, which may be strengthened or weakened by subsequent intercourse or by personally acquired knowledge of his purposes, his motives, his mentality, and his mode of action. Such impressions are of value, because unconsciously they are critical unless personal

Impressions

likes and dislikes and the sentimentality of the observer are permitted to control his judgment. Impressions, therefore, seem to be worth recording, since they will confirm, modify, or deny the popular estimate of a man by one who at least has had the opportunity of personal contact, through which the little things which enter into character are frequently disclosed, those little things which the general public cannot know and so miss an important factor in the valuation of a man's qualities of mind.

And yet it ought to be remembered that records of this sort are records of impressions rather than of reasoned opinions. They are not based on intimate association with the subject or on long and careful observation. They are not convictions gained by comparison of known facts and personal experiences. They spring from the brain without going through the slow process of analysis and deduction. Personal sentiment, to an extent, is mingled with observation and knowledge to produce an impression, and the latter is as fallible as sentiment always is when it forms the basis of opinion. In a sense, therefore, an impression is a psychological phenomenon rather than the product of the reason. It is a "snap-

Impressions

shot" of a man rather than a "time-exposure" of him. It is an outline lacking the detail of a finished portrait.

I am not sure how far an impression is affected by preconceived ideas of a man gathered from his record of achievement and his popular reputation for ability, though it is undoubtedly affected by them. Probably the influence varies in each case. But I think that it may be assumed that, if the impression conforms to a previous conception of character, the impression becomes almost a conviction; while, if it differs in marked degree from what one has been led to believe concerning a man's character, the effect is to deepen the personal satisfaction or disappointment, as the case may be, and to cause a feeling that the impression approaches nearer the truth than the evidence contradicting it, although the nature of the evidence is an important factor in determining its rejection.

This tendency to rely more upon an impression gained from personal contact, however slight, than upon popular opinion and knowledge of the previous career and accomplishments of a man, is normal. It may not be the soundest basis for accurately estimating personality, but it is very human and much more satisfying than the careful weighing of facts which are generally known. Reputations, in any event, are based not so much upon what men think and do, as upon what the world *believes* that they think and do; and, since a public estimate of a man is founded on belief, it is more easily overthrown by a personal impression than if it rested on proven facts. In many cases the personality of a man, to whom public opinion imputes greatness, assumes heroic proportions as the myth is increasingly accepted, so that a first impression, which does not conform to the public belief, is a distinct shock and disposes the observer to reject all the evidences of greatness when, in fact, only certain ones are contradicted. This is a danger which should be recognized and guarded against in valuing the recorded impressions of men. It would be folly to place them on the same plane as estimates of character founded on an analysis of established facts. They may be contributions to the general knowledge, but their worth is frequently affected by circumstance and the temper of the observer.

With these comments concerning the nature and value of personal impressions, it is my pur-

Impressions

pose to state briefly how certain men, who represented their nations at the Peace Conference at
Paris, impressed me, leaving to the reader the task
of determining the conformity or disagreement of
my impressions with the common estimate of
the characters of these men, whose careers and
public services have made them conspicuous
figures in the history of the period in which we
live.

VENIZÉLOS

No man who attended the Peace Conference aroused more general interest because of the part that he had played in the war or won more friends because of his personality than did Eleftherios Venizélos, the Greek Premier and the actual ruler of the Greek nation. I found that nearly every one was anxious to meet this leader whose personal influence had been persistently exerted until it had turned the scales in Greece against the Germans and in favor of the Allies. There was a natural curiosity to see a man who had been able to accomplish so much in spite of the difficulties that he had to overcome. Success, such as his had been in the field of international politics, confers a distinction which even the more cynical cannot ignore.

The career of M. Venizélos from his majority to his fifty-fifth year, in which he was when he attended the Peace Conference, had been a stormy one. He had been for a third of a century engaged in one rebellion after another against the Ottoman Empire which had possessed su-

ELEFTHERIOS VENIZÉLOS

zerain powers over his native island of Crete. He had more than once retired to the mountains and from their fastnesses defied the imperial authorities. He had shown a boldness in urging his demands and an inflexible spirit in the face of disappointments which made him preëminent as a patriot and as a revolutionist. Revolution with him was a creed as well as a profession. All his energies and talents had been devoted to winning the political freedom of his countrymen and the unification of the Greek people.

With the beginning of the World War his sympathies were enlisted on the side of the Allies. Whether this was due to far-seeing statesmanship or to the fact that the Ottoman Empire, against which he had been so long in conflict, was allied to the Central Powers, I do not know, but I believe that his inveterate hatred of the Turk was the chief influence which induced him to become openly active in the endeavor to persuade his country to enter the war on the side of the Allies. If they were defeated, his hope of a Greater Greece would vanish. His success in this endeavor, which he obtained only by revolt against his own Government, gained for him personally the favor of the statesmen of the

Allied Powers, so that he was able to count with
substantial certainty on their support of his aims
at the Peace Conference and to have an influential voice in the inner councils at Paris.
The views of M. Venizélos were, I believe, given
greater weight by the Big Four than those
of any other single delegate at Paris, while the
confidence which he inspired made less difficult
his task of obtaining the terms which he desired
to have inserted in the treaties with Turkey and
with Bulgaria.

In spite of the vicissitudes and hardships
which M. Venizélos had endured during his
turbulent public life, he did not look the part
of a revolutionary leader. His appearance was,
on the contrary, that of a sensitive student. He
might have been a professor in some great
European university spending his days in inter-
preting the unearthed treasures of Crete's pre-
historic civilization or in poring over faded
manuscripts containing the Hellenic philosophies
of ancient days. Of medium height and with
little superfluous flesh, with hair and beard white
and thin suggesting premature old age, M. Venizélos was not distinguished in form, feature, or
bearing. His complexion was ruddy, his eyes

bright and clear, and his mouth gentle with generous mobile lips. He stooped in walking and his attitude in standing was shrinking, almost apologetic. One could hardly avoid the feeling that here was a man too modest, if not too timid, to be a great intellectual force in world affairs, too simple of soul to mingle in the jealousies and intrigues of European politics, and too idealistic in thought to pit his mind against the material- ism and cleverness of the trained diplomats and political leaders assembled at Paris to draw a new map of Europe.

This mildness of appearance and manner was further enhanced by M. Venizélos's smile and voice. When he smiled, his whole face lighted up with benevolence and friendliness. His smile was his great charm, a charm that was empha- sized by the soft and gentle tones of his voice. Everything about him seemed to diffuse good- ness. He appeared to be living in an atmosphere of virtuous thought and kindly purpose. Imag- ination could easily picture him as patient and enduring, as the unresisting martyr of a great cause, but not as indignant and fiery, not as the intrepid leader of insurgent bands. His whole personality in fact contradicted his record.

Venizélos

Though these pronounced characteristics inspired good-will and invited sympathy and support, one could not forget what his life had been. The general impression created by his personality undoubtedly was that here was a man to be trusted implicitly, a man whose simplicity of mind and nobility of purpose would not permit him to resort to intrigue. To one, however, familiar with the shrewdness shown by M. Venizélos as Premier of Greece during the Balkan Wars and later as the head of a revolutionary government during the World War, there was the feeling that beneath his apparent innocence of craftiness existed a keen perception of strategic advantages and a readiness to seize political opportunities, which were not entirely compatible with the thoughts aroused by personal contact with him.

It seemed to me during those days at Paris that it was almost heretical to have this feeling of uncertainty as to the real character of M. Venizélos in view of the universal esteem and confidence in which he was held. The truth is that I tried to reason myself out of it, for it seemed to be inconceivable that others could be mistaken in their estimate of his qualities. The impression, nevertheless, persisted. His appearance and manner seemed to deny the facts of his career, while the knowledge of the facts would not be denied in forming an impression of the man. In a social way intercourse with him was a pleasure, but, when it came to discussing with him questions affecting Greece and to considering the statements on which he based his arguments, there was a suspicion, to say the least, of the plausible and mild-mannered Greek statesman which remained in spite of his personal attraction and the apparent genuineness of his altruism.

It is very obvious, from an examination of the terms of the Treaty of Neuilly and the Treaty of Sèvres, that M. Venizélos was successful in winning, not only the confidence, but also the active coöperation of the negotiators who represented the Allied Governments in the formulation of those documents. The settlements were wholly favorable to the Venizélos policy of "Greek unity" and to the desires of the Greek expansionists, favorable to the point of extravagance. It is not my purpose to discuss the extensive territorial acquisitions obtained by Greece under the treaties except to point out that in much of the territory the Greek populations were in the minority, particularly in Eastern Thrace and Northern Macedonia, and that there were no compensating economic or geographic reasons for the settlements. During the general discussion of the Turkish and Bulgarian peace terms, in which the American Commissioners at Paris took part, though the United States had not been at war with either country, the American position was frankly adverse to the Greek claims, not because of any unfriendliness for Greece or of friendliness for her enemies, but because the cession of areas inhabited by large hostile populations creates conditions which threaten the future peace of the world. That position was sound, as time will demonstrate.

Except for the personal influence of M. Venizélos, I am convinced that the extension of Greek sovereignty would not have been so great as it was under the treaties. What he asked was granted because *he* asked it. His personality and the reliance placed on his judgment dominated the negotiations and were sufficient to overcome the practical arguments urged against compliance with his wishes. The consequence was the creation of a new and greater Greece embracing within its territory the shores and islands of the Ægean Sea as well as Eastern Thrace, a Greece which, by uniting the Greek cities and settlements on the islands and shores of the Ægean, made of it a Greek sea, but a Greece which, by this extension of territorial sovereignty to separated coasts, became a country impossible of military defense and unstable politically on account of ethnic animosities and of lack of economic interdependence.

It is possible that my impression of M. Venizélos would have changed and been more in harmony with the common opinion of him, had it not been for this apparent appetite for territory. I found it hard to believe that a man of his experience in public affairs, and especially one who had been an active participant in the Balkan quarrels where nationality has always played a most conspicuous part, could be convinced in his own mind that it would make for the future peace and prosperity of Greece to expand her boundaries to so great an extent, since it was sure to arouse the bitter enmity of the Bulgars and Turks and invite them to war against their conquerors at the first favorable opportunity, while the defensive strength of Greece would be materially weakened, unless it became a naval power, which appeared to be substantially impossible. It seemed to be casting fresh fuel into the Balkan furnace where the fires of war are always smouldering beneath the ashes of past conflicts.

What was the reason that M. Venizélos, seemingly a sagacious and wise statesman who was keenly alive to the dangers of perpetuating the hatreds and jealousies of ambitious nationalities, adopted this policy of over-expansion of Greek territory, which even to the superficial student of world politics appeared to threaten the future peace of Southeastern Europe and the sovereignty of Greece? I do not know. It is a question which offers a field for speculation as to the motives and intellectual attainments of M. Venizélos upon which one may well hesitate to enter.

Apostle of "the unification of Greece" as he had always been, and an active agent in throwing off the yoke of alien authority from his compatriots of the island of Crete, he may have been obsessed with the idea that Greeks everywhere should be joined to the mother country by uniting under Greek sovereignty the territories where they dwell even though they are a minority of the population. The memories of Macedon and Byzantium may have inspired the hope of a new Greek Empire clothed with power and destined to revive the ancient glories of the Greek race.

It may have been that he had made promises and announced policies of an all-inclusive Greek State which he could not revoke or modify without losing prestige and political power at home, and that to retain these he was willing to risk the consequences of a course, the wisdom of which was contradicted by the logic of recent events in the history of the Balkans.

I am loath to accept this latter reason because it is open to the interpretation that M. Venizélos was willing to adopt an unwise policy in order to perpetuate his political control by satisfying the ambitions of the people of "Old Greece" and by gaining the support of the Greek inhabitants of the annexed territories. On the other hand, political promises made under the stress of impelling circumstance frequently bind men to a course of action which they would under other conditions prefer to avoid, but which they feel in honor bound to continue. It is one of the evils of opportunism which an honorable man finds hard to avoid.

If, however, the motive for the Greek Premier's urgent appeal at Paris for the union to Greece proper of the Greek-inhabited areas about the Ægean Sea and in Macedonia was his conviction that unification was for the welfare of his nation, the conclusion is that he was less wise and more visionary than he was reputed to be.

In fact, when one analyzes the record of events, there seems to be only one of two conclusions, either M. Venizélos was an unwise statesman or he was a politician who endeavored to preserve his political life by responding to the impulses of the national pride of his countrymen and of the racial affinity of those of Greek blood. In either case the popular estimate of his character is impaired.

The part played by M. Venizélos in bringing Greece into the war was made possible by the presence of Allied forces in the Saloniki region. The Greek Government had prior to that time maintained neutrality in the war, and even went so far in avoiding conflict as to permit Bulgarian occupation of Greek territory without resistance. To what extent the influence of King Constantine

Venizélos

and his German queen induced this policy is of little importance, though there can be no doubt that the Allies were disposed to credit it with chief importance. Outside of this influence, to which the pusillanimous surrender of territory gave color, the arguments in favor of a policy of neutrality were strong and convincing. Serbia, in spite of the unsurpassed valor and sacrifices of her people, had been occupied by the conquering armies of Bulgaria and Austria-Hungary. The Serbian nation had endured untold agonies at the hands of the invaders. The Allied Governments, though vigorously demanding that the Greeks aid the Serbs in the unequal struggle, would not agree to send troops or munitions to Greece, although that country was insufficiently manned and equipped to conduct a war of magnitude. In these circumstances King Constantine and his advisers declined to depart from their neutral attitude on the ground that Greece was not strong enough without foreign aid to resist the armies of the Central Alliance, and that to make war unaided and without adequate military preparations would mean that their country would suffer the fate of Serbia and the Greek people would undergo the horrors of an invasion by an utterly ruthless foe. It would seem that in the circumstances, even if the King had not been a brother-in-law of the German Emperor, the policy adopted was in the best interests of the Greek nation; and apparently the majority of the people favored this policy of neutrality.

The Allies were deeply, though I think unreasonably, incensed at this attitude of the Royal Government and sought opportunity to force Greece to take up arms against the Central Powers. Finding that M. Venizélos and his adherents, who were deeply interested in the Greeks outside of " Old Greece," were in favor of the country abandoning neutrality and taking up arms against the Central Powers, the Allied Governments finally sent forces to Saloniki and practically took possession of the port and neighboring territory in conjunction with the Greeks who favored uniting with them in the war. This action on the part of the Allies resulted in the establishment, under the leadership of M. Venizélos, of an independent Provisional Government for the Saloniki region, which increased its territorial control with the northward and eastward advance of the Allied lines. The successes of the Allies on the various battle fronts and the arrival of reënforcements in Greece seemed to prove the wisdom of the Venizélos policy of revolution, which was confirmed by his final return to political power at Athens, and the departure of the royal family from Greece.

As far as one is able to judge from the progress of events and from the subsequent restoration of Constantine to the throne, the people of "Old Greece," who had witnessed with apprehension the terrible sufferings of the Serbian nation, were never favorable to their country's abandoning its neutrality and becoming a participant in the war. The majority seemed to be opposed to the Venizélos party which held its power by grace of the Allied Governments rather than by will of the Greek nation. However, the defeat of the Bulgars, Turks, and Austrians was so complete that the Venizélos policy was vindicated and his leadership was again accepted by the nation — at least it was assumed to be accepted — and he came to the Paris Conference as the recognized master of the situation.

While the Cretan statesman, thus in control of the policies of his country through the defeat of the Central Powers, entered upon his duties as a negotiator holding the confidence and friend-

ship of the Allies because of his devotion to their
cause under doubtful, if not adverse, conditions,
he could not have been blind to the fact that
good fortune rather than popular favor had been
the means of his success, and that there smoul-
dered a fire of resentment in "Old Greece"
because, to attain his ends, he had depended on
foreign troops rather than on the will of the
Greek people. To take a conspicuous place in the
deliberations at Paris and to employ the good-
will of the Allies for the extension of the territorial possessions of Greece must have seemed to
him a wise course to pursue, as there was reason
to believe that attainment of his object would
satisfy the national aspirations and win the favor
of many who had opposed the abandonment of
neutrality and who had resented his revolutionary act in forcing King Constantine to
abandon his throne.

The knowledge of M. Venizélos's career doubtless affected the impression that he made upon
me, although that impression was decidedly at
variance with the sort of man whom I had expected to meet. In spite of the fact that he had
been in repeated revolts against constituted
authority and had lived as an outlaw in the

mountains of Crete, he was, as I have stated, in appearance, in manner, and seemingly in temperament, the opposite of a typical revolutionist, especially of a Greek revolutionist whom popular imagination pictures as a swarthy, passionate brigand bristling with weapons. To accept this mild-mannered, soft-voiced gentleman, whose gentle eyes looked through his gold-rimmed spectacles with a most benignant expression and whose lips curved in the kindliest of smiles, as the stern, inflexible revolutionist, under whose leadership Crete had cast off Moslem rule and the devotees of "New Greece" had arisen against the Government of Athens, seemed to deny the evidence of one's own senses. Thus facts came into direct conflict with the impression which his personality made upon one who had actual intercourse with him and affected the impression in a peculiar way.

The effect was to cause one to feel that the true Venizélos was hidden; and that his suavity, his modesty, his soft voice and gentleness were not real. The unavoidable impression was that beneath all this apparent simplicity and frankness there was a shrewd and clever politician, who, watching from the ambush of outward appearance the progress of the negotiations, was prepared to take advantage of every opportunity to serve the cause of "Greater Greece," of which he sought to be the creator as he was the apostle.

It is not agreeable to admit this impression of the great Cretan, because it is at variance with the popular judgment of the nobility of his character and the unselfishness of his purpose. In spite of my liking for M. Venizélos, a liking which I am sure was shared by every delegate to the Peace Conference whose national interests did not clash with those of Greece, I could not avoid the impression that, in the endeavor to accomplish his aims for his nation and for his own political future, he was disposed to adopt the methods of Balkan diplomacy, in which he had proven himself an adept, and which are supposed to be by no means as scrupulous and free from deception as the highest standard of statesmanship required of a negotiator.

Yet, in stating this impression of the character and personal qualities of Eleftherios Venizélos, I cannot deny that it is done with hesitation and with a measure of uncertainty. The sentimental and rational points of view are strangely antagonistic. My impression may be wrong. It would be a real gratification to find that it was, because I would like to feel that the attractive personality of the Venizélos whom I knew was the personality of the real Venizélos, and that there was nothing beneath the surface, nothing hidden in his thought and purpose, which contradicted the openness of his manner and the candor of his words. It is not easy with a man of such personal charm to doubt his sincerity of conduct or to question the ideals which seemed to influence him. To do so is to deny the evidence of personal feelings, a denial which a man is loath to make. For that reason it has been a hard task to give my actual impression of the Greek Premier, whose career as a delegate to the Peace Conference was brilliant and successful and whose personal attainments and achievements have won for him universal praise throughout the nations opposed to the Central Powers. While subsequent events have caused amazement and aroused queries as to how far M. Venizélos truly represented the Greek people, the impression which I gained of him during our sojourn in Paris has not been materially affected, though his rejection in the elections of 1921 made me feel less doubtful of the correctness of my own thoughts regarding him, which I could not suppress while I was in Paris or later when the Treaty of Sèvres was being negotiated.

In a way the personality of M. Venizélos remains an enigma which cannot be solved until years have passed and one can look back over the history of this period unaffected by the present chaotic state of Southeastern Europe and by the passions unloosed in this World War. Only with these events as a background can the actors stand out in their true perspective. To-day the impression is vivid, but its accuracy or inaccuracy will only be disclosed by time when the critical historian and biographer are uninfluenced by the little things which are so potent in the forming of contemporary opinions of character.

EMIR FEISUL

THE impression made by the physical qualities of a man and that made by his intellectual attainments are not always easy to dissociate, nor is it easy to give them their relative value in the estimating of character. Undoubtedly a first impression is due to the sense of sight and is modified or removed only when association furnishes opportunity to know and measure a man's mentality and the spirit and motives which lie behind his words and thoughts.

Physical attractions and agreeable manners may make a favorable impression, but this impression may vanish, if beneath the pleasing exterior of a man there is discovered a mind tainted with viciousness, weakness, or unworthy purpose. On the other hand, a man may be unattractive or insignificant in appearance, without grace of manner, even uncouth, but withal the possessor of lofty sentiments and of intellectual talents which cause one to forget his physical defects and to see only the finer qualities of his nature.

Emir Feisul

Nevertheless, the influence of visual sensations cannot be ignored in the attempt to analyze an impression of a man's personality. Those sensations, even when denied by previous knowledge or by reason, are apt to persist, and to affect to a degree an opinion founded on more substantial grounds. If the impression, subsequently acquired through mental processes, confirms the verdict of the senses, the impression becomes deeper and more certain. When the physical and intellectual qualities seem to be entirely in harmony, an observer feels that his first impression is a true estimate of character, an estimate which only the most convincing evidence can change.

This attempt to look back to the sources of impressions, and to determine the standard of relative value to be applied to them, is induced by the thought of the Emir Feisul, the Prince of the Hedjaz. The vivid picture of this distinguished Arabian that arose in my mind as I thought of him caused me to realize that an unerasable impression had been made upon me by his physical characteristics, his bearing and his dress, as well as the impression made by his mental qualities. From which did I gain the most? Did one impression modify the other? It

[162]

Harris & Ewing, Washington, D.C.

EMIR FEISUL

Emir Feisul

was in analyzing these factors of the problem
that I realized that, when they were not at variance, they blended into one which was stronger
and deeper because of this unity.

Of the many prominent representatives of
races, nationalities, and creeds, who gathered in
Paris to negotiate the treaties of peace and to
restore, as far as possible, the political and social
order shattered by the war, there was none more
striking in appearance than this prince from the
Sacred City, where the mysteries of Islam were
so long guarded from Christendom by the deserts
of Arabia and the fanaticism of the followers of
the Prophet. Slender and erect, seeming to be
taller than he actually was, his flowing black
robe and golden turban, with a richly embroid-
ered veil falling gracefully over his shoulders
from beneath the turban's edge, enhanced his
calm dignity of carriage and the serious expression which never left his face. No one could look
at the Emir Feisul without the instinctive feeling
that here was a man whom nature had chosen
to be a leader of men, a man who was worthy to
be a leader of men.

The features of the Arab Prince were clear-cut,
regular, and typical of his race. His hair and

beard were black and slightly curling. His lips, which were partially hidden by a small mustache, were red and full, but did not indicate grossness or sensuality. His complexion was sallow and slightly mottled like the majority of those of pure Semitic blood. His face was thin and, though with few lines and wrinkles, was strong and earnest in expression. His dark eyes were serene and kindly, but one could easily imagine that they would flash fire under the excitement of conflict or the impulse of violent emotion. Candor and truth were in the straightforward look from his eyes. He had none of that subtlety of expression, that ill-concealed craftiness, which is so often characteristic of the facial lines of the natives of Southwestern Asia.

The movements of the Emir Feisul were always unhurried and stately. He moved and spoke with deliberation and dignity. One felt his reserve power and his strength of character, while there was the feeling that he possessed a profundity of thought which raised him above the common man. He suggested the calmness and peace of the desert, the meditation of one who lives in the wide spaces of the earth, the solemnity of thought of one who often communes

alone with nature. Everything about the Emir
commanded respect. In him one seemed to see
nobility of character and nobility of purpose.
That was the impression that he made upon me
when I first saw the picturesque chieftain of the
Hedjaz, and that is the impression that remained
unchanged when I came to know him better
and to appreciate the intellectual force which
harmonized so entirely with his physical characteristics.

Though Prince Feisul was comparatively
young in years, he showed a maturity of judgment and a self-restraint which one does not
usually associate with youth, at least not with
the youth of our Western World. In appearance and address he might have been one of the
prophets of ancient days with his burden of
foreknowledge and with his divinely imposed
task to proclaim it to his fellow-men. There was
also about him, though not out of accord with his
prophetic type, the suggestion of the chivalry of
the days when the wealth and culture of the
world were gathered in the cities of Baghdad and
Cordova, and when the Saracen Caliphs were
the great patrons of art and learning. He
seemed to belong to the age when Islam had

attained the zenith of its power and magnificence, as well as to the age of the Israelite kings.

Yet with the dual suggestion of an ancient seer and a Moslem paladin this Arabian was not wanting in modern thought and ways. He had led his army of one hundred thousand men northward from Mecca and Medina, and, employing all the enginery and art of modern warfare, had coöperated successfully with the British against the Turkish forces. He had proven himself a skillful general, a strategist of no mean ability, and above all a master in the control of the rude Bedouin tribes who fought under his banner and to whom the discipline of modern troops was normally distasteful. However wild and untrained the nomad bands who flocked to his standard, he was able to weld them into a fighting machine which was of material aid to his British allies in driving out of Palestine and Syria the veteran forces of the Ottoman Empire, whose excellence as soldiers has long been proverbial. His military record is an enviable one, and in dealing with civilians he exhibited the same forcefulness and sagacity that characterized his career as a martial leader.

But the achievements of the Arab Prince were

Emir Feisul

not due to his ability alone. The task of forming and directing the armies of the Hedjaz was shared by Colonel Thomas Lawrence, the young British archæologist, who, abandoning the researches in which he was engaged, became the chief adviser of the Emir in preparing the Arabs to wage war against the Ottoman Empire and his efficient lieutenant in the conduct of military operations. And yet, while Colonel Lawrence is entitled to a generous share in the praise for all that was accomplished, the fact in no way lessens the credit due to the Emir Feisul for the success of the Arab arms. It was about him, a Moslem, that the tribesmen gathered. It was for his sake that they rushed into battle against the Turks. He was the personification of a cause, the living inspiration to Arab unity and independence. Without him success would have been impossible. But success resulted from the combined efforts of these two talented men; the one, the sagacious Moslem leader of his countrymen; the other, the wise British counselor and faithful friend of the Arabs.

The Emir Feisul came to the Peace Conference with the purpose, and I believe with the expectation, of founding an Arab kingdom extending northward from the desert wastes of the Arabian Peninsula to the Taurus Mountains and the borders of old Armenia, and from the Euphrates to the Mediterranean. The vast majority of the inhabitants of this region were of Arabian and Aramean stocks and with few exceptions believers in the Koran. The capital of this new state was to be Damascus, the royal city of the ancient Kingdom of Syria, which was so powerful and important in the time when Samaria was the capital of Israel. The Emir's desire seems to have been to include Palestine within the boundaries of the proposed state, a not unreasonable desire in view of the fact that nearly nine tenths of the population of that territory are to-day of Arab blood, though I think that he could not have been sanguine of achieving this wish in view of the Zionist Movement which had received the unqualified support of the British Government.

He presented the Arab claim and the aspirations of the Mahommedans of Syria before the Council of Ten of the Peace Conference. Unquestionably he impressed his hearers strongly with the soundness of his arguments and with the calm and judicial way in which he gave his reasons for the rebirth of Syria as an independent state. Without gestures and without evidence of emotion, yet with an earnestness which gave great weight to his words, the unfamiliar Arabic fell from his lips to be caught up by his skilled interpreters and converted into English and French phrases. The Prince spoke with solemn dignity, perhaps it would be more accurate to say with stateliness, and with an ease of utterance which denoted familiarity in addressing public assemblages. One longed to be able to understand the language which he used, for there is no doubt that his sentences lost much through translation, particularly in the vividness of expression where the Arabic idiom found no direct counterpart in the European tongues. But even with this handicap to a perfect submission of his case, his manner of address and the tones of voice seemed to breathe the perfume of frankincense and to suggest the presence of richly colored divans, green turbans, and the glitter of gold and jewels.

As the slender Arab stood before the Council in his flowing robe and curiously wrought headdress with his fine features and serene expression, he looked the Oriental monarch that he aspired to be. One could easily imagine him to be the reincarnation of Haroun al Raschid, one fitted to be the Caliph of the new Caliphate of Damascus, who personified the union of our present civilization with the traditions and splendors of a thousand years ago.

But the Emir Feisul met in Paris forces more powerful and less easy to overcome than the Turkish armies against which he had battled so successfully. There had existed for generations throughout the Christian world an antipathy toward the Mahommedan faith, which had found evil expression in the tyranny of Turkish rule and in the unspeakable atrocities perpetrated by the Tartars of Asia and the fanatical tribesmen of the Soudan. The savagery and depravity of modern Islam had become intolerable. The Christian nations only sought opportunity to free the Christians of those regions from the degraded state to which they had fallen through centuries of Moslem oppression. The collapse of the Ottoman Empire offered this opportunity and the European delegates to the Paris Conference were generally determined to prevent a restoration of the power of the Mussulman in the territories which had been subject to the sovereignty of the Sultan and a prey to the villainies of Turkish officials.

This atmosphere of hostility to Moslem rule made the purpose of the Emir Feisul to create a new Kingdom of Syria — which, remember, was to be a new Moslem kingdom — difficult of accomplishment. While it was recognized that there was every reason to believe that there would be a great difference between a Turkish government and an Arab government, the feeling persisted that the teachings of the Koran, interpreted as they had been by the " unspeakable Turk," offered little promise of toleration of other religions, especially of Christianity. Had it been a question of the revival of the Ottoman Empire within its old frontiers, there would have been no discussion. The Conference was emphatically opposed to such a revival. But the creation of a new Arab state was different. It was a new idea and introduced a new element into the problem of territorial adjustments in the Near East. In fact the important part played by the Arabs in the conflict against the Turks and the antagonism existing between the Kingdom of the Hedjaz and the Sultan's Empire offered the possibility of destroying the unity of the Moslem world and breaking down the movement of Pan-Islamism which was a growing menace to the peace of Asia. So appealing was this policy from a political point of view, especially when it was urged by Prince Feisul, whose personality won him friends on every hand, that it might have succeeded in overcoming the common sentiment against the erection of a Moslem-ruled Syria if it had not been for other forces exerted against its adoption.

These other forces were less worthy than the desire to free the Christians of Syria and the Jews of Palestine from the tyranny and oppression of Moslem governors. They were the ambitions of some of the Great Powers and the jealousies which existed between them as to their respective influence and commercial advantages in the Near East. France, the historic champion of the Christians of The Lebanon, had looked forward to obtaining control of Syria when the Turkish Empire was broken up. French sentiment, as well as the prospect of material benefit, demanded Syria; and this had been agreed to by Great Britain, while France had agreed that the British share of the spoils should be the rich valleys of Mesopotamia and also Palestine, the proposed national home for the Jews. The acceptance of the idea of an independent Syria under Arab sovereignty would destroy this agreement, and turn the coveted territories over to a government which might prevent the exploitation of their resources by the powers which had long realized their economic possibilities.

While the British Government might have listened with a friendly ear to the proposals of the Emir except those in conflict with the promises made to the Zionists concerning Palestine, the French Government was unequivocally opposed to Arab control. The suggestion of such a disposition of Syria seemed to arouse their indignation. They declared that it could not be for a moment considered, that the division of that portion of dismembered Turkey had been definitely arranged during the progress of the war, and that they did not propose to compel the freed Christians to submit again to the fanatical oppression and cruelty of Moslem rulers. Though the sentimental reason of protecting Christians was urged with frequency and vigor, it was almost impossible to avoid the suspicion that material interests had a decided effect on the French position. Probably, too, the fact

that the Arabs had coöperated with the British
forces in the Near East caused the belief that
Syria as an independent Arab state would be
subject chiefly to British influence and open a
field for British enterprise and investment, a
field which the French had the anticipation of
dominating. A possible conflict of interests, im-
pairing a possible benefit, apparently induced
France to repudiate the thought of a new Kingdom of Syria.

The emissary of the Arabian people, the
spokesman of the Moslems, who so vastly out-
numbered the Syrians of other creeds, could do
nothing against these influences. He failed in his
mission to Paris, and his failure has passed into
history. Great Britain and France denied independence to the Syrian Arabs, and, when Prince
Feisul later attempted to assume the throne of
Syria, they compelled him by force or the menace
of force to abandon the adventure, while they
took over the government and nominated themselves as mandatories under the League of Nations in accordance with the Sykes-Picot Agreement.

One cannot look forward to the future of
Syria without apprehension or without question-

Emir Feisul

ing the political stability of the treaty settlements. Will the great body of Moslem Syrians remain satisfied and content or will they in the future become ardent supporters of Pan-Islamism and rise in rebellion against their Christian rulers, delivering the scepter to the man who so faithfully represented them against their Turkish oppressors and so eloquently advocated Syrian independence before the Peace Conference? Is there to be no more uncertainty, no further change in the sovereignty? The unbidden thought arises that it may not be long before war again sweeps across the rich valleys and barren wildernesses which lie between the shores of the Mediterranean and the banks of the Euphrates. The seeds of discontent and hatred have been sown in fertile soil; it needs but time and preparation under the direction of a masterful and resourceful leader for those seeds to germinate and to bear the bitter fruit of conflict.

It may seem that I have gone far afield from the impression made upon me by the Emir Feisul at Paris in setting forth the difficulties and discouragements which surrounded him, but the impression of his personality was materially affected by his attitude in the environment of the

Emir Feisul

Peace Conference, which was so unfavorable to the cause which he represented. The manner of the man in the circumstances was so admirable that his dignity and poise were emphasized and made a deeper impression because he was striving against irresistible forces. It was a test of character and of temperament which enhanced the high regard in which he was held by the delegates to the Conference.

Prince Feisul made the impression of one who combined the best and finest traits of Oriental character. Nobility and dignity, honesty and candor, reserve and wisdom, were manifest in his conduct and words. Whatever may have been the merits of his claims and purposes, — and as to those merits there may be from the standpoints of principle and policy sincere differences of opinion, — no one who came into personal contact with the Arabian leader could feel aught but regret for him personally in the failure of his mission. He seemed so eminently fitted for success even though he was of a religion that has been a curse rather than a blessing in so many lands. One could not but wonder if Pan-Islam with its perils to international peace would not have been swept away had an independent

Emir Feisul

Kingdom of Syria been erected with a ruler hostile to the Turks and friendly, if not grateful, to the Christian Powers. With Feisul on the throne would not the peace of the Near East have been more secure and the menace of the Ottomans been forever ended?

NOTE. — Since the foregoing " impression " was written, the British Government holding the mandate over Mesopotamia directed a tribal referendum on the selection of a king over that territory, with the result that Feisul was overwhelmingly elected. He was immediately proclaimed "King of Irak" and formally recognized as such by Great Britain at the city of Baghdad, the capital of the new Arab state.

GENERAL BOTHA

ANOTHER delegate to the Peace Conference who made a strong impression upon me was General Louis Botha, the Premier of the South African Union, who with General Jan C. Smuts represented the united colonies in the large group of delegates which participated in the proceedings at Paris on behalf of the British Empire. Unfortunately for South Africa and for the Imperial Government, General Botha died soon after his return to his country. It is deplorable that he was not spared to carry on the work of racial unity which he had so effectively championed for over a decade and which promises so much for the future prosperity of the white population of South Africa.

No one could talk with General Botha without being immediately struck by the fact that his outstanding mental quality was practical and unalloyed common sense. He was not lacking in imagination or in ideals, — his whole public career denied such a lack, — but he measured his ideals and constructive purposes by the standard

General Botha

of practicability and valued them accordingly. I
am sure that he viewed untried political theories
with suspicion and had to be convinced that they
could be reduced to working formulæ before he
gave to them his actual support. In fact he told
me so. He was essentially logical and unemotional in whatever he said and whatever he did.
The enthusiasm of the visionary made no head-
way with him. Reason and facts were what
appealed to him.

His knowledge of human nature, gained
through twenty years of conflict and in readjust-
ment of the relations between nationalities in
South Africa, was a great asset to him in the
determination of the wise and politic course to
pursue. He seemed to know what the effect of
adopting this or that policy would be. He looked
forward to the final judgment of men and not to
the temporary popularity which a policy might
gain under the stress of existing conditions or the
passing emotions of an aroused public opinion.
He possessed that foresight which sees the end at
the beginning and prevents the adoption of a
course which may be disastrous or unwise or of
doubtful expediency.

I think the impression that most persons

gained of General Botha on first acquaintance
with him, unless familiar with his career, was that
his mind worked slowly and that he was slow
in grasping the essential features of a subject
under discussion. It took, however, but a brief
time to remove this impression. Any one at all
observant soon realized that his mind was excep-
tionally keen, though he was deliberate in forming his conclusions and cautious in giving his
opinions to others. He thought out a problem to
the end before he spoke; and when he did speak
his words were carefully chosen and expressed
his views with exactness.

Throughout a discourse on a serious subject
General Botha exhibited his regard for practicality. There was an entire absence of emotion and
of levity. He was positive, but never vehement
in speaking. He avoided sentimental appeals,
but he did not ignore or undervalue the psychological effect of a proposed policy upon others.
He appreciated the importance of sentiment as
a force in public affairs, but he never apparently
permitted his own emotions to be so stirred
that they interfered with his forming an opinion
based solely upon reason. The impassioned
eloquence of an orator did not, in my judgment,

swerve him a hair's breadth from the cold logic of actual facts. I cannot conceive him to have been affected by such influences. It would have been contrary to his very nature. He was a poor "subject" for visionaries to attempt to impress with their hypnotic arts.

This marked characteristic of the South African leader's mentality had been evinced throughout his public life. It had had much to do with his having attained so high a place among his countrymen and with their recognition of his ability. As one of the younger Boer generals — he was only thirty-six years old at the time of the South African War — he had risen from the ranks to be commander-in-chief of the Transvaal armies. With dauntless spirit he had led his sturdy compatriots against the vastly superior forces of the British and in the years of unequal conflict had shown himself a tireless and skillful military leader. When it became evident beyond question that the Boer cause was hopeless, General Botha, with the common sense which characterized his acts, accepted defeat as final, and labored for peace even though it meant the surrender to the British Crown of the sovereignty of the Boer Republics. This was no easy or

agreeable undertaking, for he had to persuade
the fierce old chieftain of the Orange Free State,
General De Wet, to submit to the inevitable.
That he succeeded was due to the cogency of
his arguments as to the hopelessness, and, therefore, the folly, of continuing the struggle against
the superior might of the British Empire. General De Wet and the crippled but indomitable
Steyne, the President of the southern Boer Republic, sullenly consented to the peace which deprived their country of its national life, though
in their retirement following the war they cherished the hope that the future would offer opportunity to regain their national independence.

General Botha, on the other hand, had a
different vision and a different hope for South
Africa. Realizing that it was for the interests
of his own people to live in amity with their
neighbors of British blood and that the restoration of Boer independence was practically impossible, even if desirable, he determined to
weld the white populations of South Africa into
one people independent to all intents, though
acknowledging the sovereignty of the British
Crown. How well he and those who aided him
in this endeavor succeeded is a fact of history.

General Botha

A less broad-minded and far-seeing statesman than the Transvaal general would have kept alive a spirit of revenge among his countrymen and counseled passive resistance to the British authorities, thus making amalgamation between the two nationalities a long and painful process. That would have been a very natural course to take. It would have conformed with the common conception of patriotism and the usual sentiment of the vanquished toward the victors, but it did not conform with General Botha's views as to what was wise and practical. He may have regretted, and doubtless did regret, the outcome of the war, in which he had been a prominent military figure, but he did not permit vain regrets or false hopes to cloud his vision as to the future or to impair his sound common sense in dealing with new conditions resulting from the British victory. He knew that the South African Republic and the Orange Free State could never regain their independence. He accepted the fact of defeat with philosophic calmness and exerted all his influence as a popular commander in reconciling his fellow-countrymen to their new allegiance.

His efforts did not cease with inducing the

majority of the Boers to adjust themselves to the idea of British rule, for in seeking the welfare of the inhabitants of the conquered republics he began at once the movement for union of all the South African colonies into a self-governing dominion of the British Empire. In this he was aided by the statesmen of Great Britain, who realized the tremendous advantage to be gained by a political union creating common interests and making possible common action by the white race in South Africa. The successful organization of the Union was largely due to General Botha, and his elevation to the premiership was a recognition of his wise statesmanship.

He was engaged in breaking down the last barriers of hostile feeling between the two nationalities, and in working out an ambitious programme of development and expansion for the Union, when the European War broke out. The situation put to the test his loyalty and wisdom and the strength of the unity for which he had labored. The military demands upon Great Britain in Belgium and Northern France and the presence of German troops in Southwest Africa seemed to offer a favorable opportunity to the unreconciled Boers to recover their in-

dependence and possibly to occupy Cape Colony
and Natal. A less sagacious statesman than
General Botha, and one less appreciative of the
great issues at stake in the war, would, in the
circumstances, have raised the standard of revolt
against British rule. But the Boer Premier never
hesitated in his decision or faltered in his allegiance. He preferred a course which did not
violate his sense of honor and which did not
endanger the political liberty and equal justice
enjoyed by all South Africans as British subjects,
irrespective of their nationality. He not only
supported with his voice the cause of the battling
Allies, but he informed the London Government
that they might withdraw for service in Europe
the troops stationed in South Africa, assuring
them that the Colonial Government would be
responsible for the loyalty and defense of the
territory. The confidence reposed in the integrity of the Boer leader by the British Government was shown by the advantage which was
immediately taken of this offer. The British
garrisons embarked for England.

In spite of the fine spirit shown by General
Botha in this crisis, there were many among the
Boers who had continued to cherish a feeling

of hatred toward the British and to dream of a return to their former state of independence. To this dissatisfied group the occupied energies of the Empire in the life-and-death struggle in Flanders offered a temptation to cast off their enforced allegiance. As a consequence of this spirit and these conditions, an insurrection broke out in the United Colonies, the insurrectionists undertaking to seize the local governments at various points. The colonial forces, which General Botha had organized, were sent against the rebels, and they were, with little bloodshed, overcome and dispersed. At the head of the movement was the veteran commander-in-chief of the Orange Free State, General De Wet, who had never favored the Botha policy of union and who was an inveterate hater of the British. His capture in the deserts of Bechuanaland by loyal troops brought the rebellion to an end, while the amnesty granted the rebels prevented them from becoming martyrs in the eyes of their country-men and destroyed the possibility of a revival of the movement for independence.

As soon as the rebels at home had been sup-pressed, General Botha led his colonial forces into German Southwest Africa overcoming the garri-

General Botha

sons in that territory and raising over the colony
the Union Jack of the British Empire in place of
the Black Eagle of Prussia.

General Jan C. Smuts saw the situation as
General Botha saw it. He was the latter's
faithful lieutenant in the field as he had been in
the movement for union and in the political
administration of the country. It was the sound
judgment and prompt action of these two 'Boer
statesmen and generals which saved South
Africa from a civil war which would have caused
much suffering and loss to the colonists and re-
awakened all the antipathy and bitterness between the nationalities which had been rapidly
disappearing under the leadership of Louis
Botha. But their statesmanship went further
than that. They looked beyond the boundaries
and coasts of South Africa, and without hesitation showed that they preferred to stand side
by side with the men who, but a few years before,
had conquered them and annexed their country,
but had given them political liberty, rather than
to stand against them and support the Prussians
in their designs of world empire. It was a big-
hearted, a large-minded, a noble decision. It is
an example of the highest type of statesmanship.

It makes famous the names of Louis Botha and Jan C. Smuts in the annals of the World War. The conduct of these two great Boers in this critical time should not be forgotten when we recall the acts which excite our admiration and praise and which are worthy to be remembered by posterity. How eminently proper it was that they should represent South Africa at Paris.

Both General Botha and General Smuts impressed me as belonging to the class of men popularly termed " sound and substantial." There was a simplicity of manner, an absence of affectation, a frankness of speech, an intellectual honesty about them, that appealed strongly to one who came in contact with them. You trusted them because you knew instinctively that they were worthy of your trust. They seemed to lack the art of dissimulation, so that they were distinguished from the many adepts in that art to be found among the delegates to the Peace Conference. They spoke their minds freely without attempting to soften the truth or to make it more palatable, and yet their attitude was one of kindliness and consideration. General Botha — and I am disposed to add General Smuts, though with less certainty — belonged to the type of public men who develop under the plain conditions of pioneer life and the constant struggle against primitive nature. It is a fine type; in many ways the finest type. To that type belonged Abraham Lincoln.

While I have considered General Botha and General Smuts together, because their public lives were to an extent formed by the same experience and consequently possessed many characteristics in common, they were by no means identical in certain of their attributes and attainments. General Smuts, educated at one of the great English universities, was undoubtedly more cultured, and possessed a more far-reaching imagination than his great leader. Some would possibly say that he had a wider vision. I prefer to call it imagination. He worked out, prior to the assembling of the Peace Conference, a plan for a League of Nations which became the basis of the plan adopted in the Treaty of Versailles. This plan furnishes an excellent example of his mental caliber as a constructive political thinker.

I do not believe that General Botha, with his high regard for practicality and his unwillingness to adopt a political theory which had not been tested by actual application, would have pre-

General Botha

sented a plan like that proposed by General
Smuts. He possessed foresight rather than an
adventurous imagination. He had his ideals,
but he was not an idealist. He had vision, but he
was not a visionary. It is hard to explain just
the distinction that I would convey between his
mentality and that of his colleague. Perhaps it
may be stated to be the difference between a
theory which is *certainly* practicable and a theory
which is *possibly* practicable. Perhaps it can be
expressed by the difference between the assertion
that two and two make four if past experience
applies, and the assertion that two and two may,
if an unusual theory is accepted, make five. In
any event, the attempt to define the distinction
between the intellectual processes of these two
men involves a subtlety of thought which is
difficult to put into exact terms.

In comparing the impressions made upon me
by the two Boer statesmen, I realize that that
made by General Botha was much more positive and much stronger than that made by
General Smuts. While this was due in no small
degree to the fact that I saw General Botha frequently and had little intercourse with General
Smuts, I think that it was influenced by the

General Botha

belief that General Botha's character seemed to me the stronger of the two. He did not have the vivacity of mind which comes with a restless imagination. He kept his feet on the ground and dealt with certainties rather than with possibilities. He did not stumble because he was not constantly gazing at the stars. Some would have called him commonplace. Doubtless many did call him so in thought if not in word. I think that those who so judged him mistook the commonplace for a plainness born of common sense.

From his experience of men and things and from his discerning knowledge of that undefinable but all-pervading quality which we term human nature, General Botha obtained his conclusions, and on these conclusions he built his judgments or by them guided his course of action. His sentiments never diverted the current of his reason. It was a steady, uninterrupted flow which was well-nigh irresistible. His logic was cold, exact, and unemotional. The soundness and clarity of his thought carried conviction.

An example of the way in which General Botha's practical common sense dominated his feelings was furnished by his attitude toward the articles in the Treaty of Versailles providing for the political trial of the former German Emperor and his officers upon charges of responsibility for beginning the war and for the atrocious and inhuman acts perpetrated by the German soldiery during the invasion of Belgium and France. Though he frankly stated his loathing for these men and his indignation at the abominable wrongs committed by their orders or with their apparent approval, he strongly opposed their punishment by the Allies, because he was convinced that, if they were punished, the German people would canonize them as national martyrs and cherish in their hearts a spirit of hatred and revenge toward their judges which would ultimately bring about another war. The astute South African statesman, who knew from personal experience the spirit and temper of a vanquished people, was willing and in fact intensely anxious to abandon the infliction of just penalties on these violators of international peace and the laws of humanity, because he knew that abandonment of punishments would make the peace more enduring by removing the incentive to retaliate. So strongly was he convinced of this course that he said to me one day, when we were lunching together, that his conscience and reason told him not to sign the treaty, which had then been delivered to the German delegates, unless the articles providing for penalties were expunged. For a long time he remained, to my knowledge, uncertain as to his duty, and he determined to affix his signature to the document only when he was convinced that his refusal might produce a greater evil by delaying the restoration of peace and by encouraging the radical elements in the Central Empires to attempt to seize the governments at Berlin and Vienna. He was not alone in being compelled by the logic of the situation, which made Bolshevism a very real peril, to subordinate his personal convictions and inclinations and to make choice between two evils.

In this rational attitude toward the danger of perpetuating hatreds and resentments by the terms of peace, General Botha was closely followed by General Smuts, but I believe that this sane view of the policy which ought to be adopted originated with General Botha. The private conversations which I had with him, concerning the subject of punishing individuals, showed an earnest opposition to such a course, even before the insistence of Mr. Lloyd George, for political reasons, and of the French, out of a very natural spirit of retaliation, had forced the articles on penalties to be written into the Treaty of Versailles.

Physically General Botha was a large, strongly built man, with a tendency toward heaviness which made him rather slow and clumsy in his movements. He had a decidedly Dutch cast of countenance with roundness of face, high cheekbones, and few wrinkles. His hair, mustache, and imperial were dark, as were his eyes. His mouth was wide with thick lips. His teeth, which were neither white nor even, were large and very much in evidence when he smiled or talked. His simplicity of dress and manner was conspicuous. In conversation he always spoke in a straightforward way with little emphasis. There was nothing in his voice which distinguished it from that of the average man. He used a simple vocabulary and used it well, speaking, however, with a slight accent. He possessed humor rather than wit. He was an excellent talker, having a fund of anecdotes of South African life and personal experiences which he related in an entertaining manner. When he ventured to speculate on the future and its problems, his

General Botha

listener could not but feel that his foundation
was laid in facts and that he based his deductions
on sound premises. There was a practicality
about his utterances, an avoidance of extremes,
and an accuracy of reasoning which made his
deductions of unusual value.

Louis Botha impressed me as a soldier who
hated war and abhorred militarism, and as a
statesman without vanity or personal ambition,
whose principal characteristics were honesty of
purpose, unaffected simplicity of manner, and
candor of address. For him to engage in intrigue
or to act unjustly was unthinkable. His patriotism was not of the emotional type which acted
on impulse and bubbled over with uncontrolled
enthusiasm. It was deeper and more earnest and
more useful to his country than the frothy type,
for it was founded on an abiding faith in his
fellow-men and in a love of humanity which
tempered justice with mercy and a sense of
personal wrong with a spirit of forgiveness. His
long and active public career with its record of
achievement is ample justification for any en-
comium that may be paid to his memory.
Through his death the Union of South Africa lost
its greatest statesman and the British Empire

one of its wisest counselors and most loyal leaders at a time when his cool and sober judgment were especially needed, and when the universal confidence and respect in which he was held by his people would have exerted a powerful influence in bringing into complete unity the two nationalities in South Africa, to accomplish which had been the ambition of his life, the hope that had inspired his public service.

PADEREWSKI

AMONG the statesmen who assembled in Paris in December, 1918, to formulate the terms of peace to be imposed on the defeated Powers of Central Europe, Ignace Jan Paderewski, the Minister for Foreign Affairs and the Premier of the new-born Republic of Poland, was a notable figure, not only because of his personality, but because he represented a country which, through its fortitude and faith in spite of the inconceivable agonies which its people endured during the war, had won back its national life and independence torn from it over a hundred years ago by the greed and jealousies of the two Central Powers and Russia. The partition of the ancient Kingdom of Poland, which had been so powerful in Eastern Europe during the seventeenth century, but which had been weakened by internal dissensions and by the foreign intrigues of its political factions, is a dark page in the history of modern civilization. The dismemberment of so large and populous a territory possessing solidarity in race, language, and religion, such as Poland possessed, was an international crime which hardly finds a parallel in the annals of the past four hundred years.

In spite, however, of the submergence of the Poles as a nation for a century and the persistent efforts of their conquerors to break their spirit of national entity, they transmitted from generation to generation the hope that they would again be a sovereign people, and that the broken pieces of their country would be reunited so that Poland might again take her place as a member of the family of nations. With this hope a living force in binding the Polish people together, they tenaciously clung to their language, their creed, their traditions, and above all to their hatred of the domination of those who had deprived them of their national existence.

The result of the World War made possible the realization of this constant hope. The opportunity had come to consummate it. With this supreme end in view, Poland sent to Paris Ignace Paderewski and Roman Dmowski to negotiate the terms to be incorporated in the peace treaties and in a treaty of Poland with the principal Powers. Their task, in spite of the sympathetic attitude of the Allies and the United States, was not an easy one. There were

Paderewski

very difficult problems to be solved in the delimitation of the frontiers of Poland, for her territory, while she was an independent state, had been a variable quantity, since her borders had fluctuated with the triumph or failure of her arms in the wars in which the Poles were almost incessantly engaged during the sixteenth, seventeenth, and eighteenth centuries. At what period in Polish history did the boundaries enclose Poland proper? What ethnic and economic considerations must enter into the determination of the new boundaries? These were questions, the answers to which were vital, not only to the future of Poland, but also to the future peace of Eastern Europe and to the stability of the settlements under the treaties. In formulating these answers Mr. Paderewski took a leading part, and, though naturally prejudiced in favor of extending Polish sovereignty to the limit of her historic possessions, he was not unmindful of the great underlying idea that the new Poland must be a state possible of military defense as well as of an independent economic life.

In looking back over the years of the war and the months succeeding the signing of the armistice on November 11, 1918, I realize that I had two distinct, and to an extent contradictory, impressions made upon me by Mr. Paderewski. The first impression was that which I gained in the United States while the war was in progress, an impression which was superseded and substantially extinguished by a later impression which resulted from a more intimate acquaintance with the Polish statesman and which was confirmed by his record at Warsaw and at Paris.

My original impression was not one of a complimentary nature in view of the task which he had undertaken in behalf of his country. It was due undoubtedly to the fact that he was a great pianist, the greatest, I believe, of his generation. I felt that his artistic temperament, his passionate devotion to music, his intense emotions, and his reputed eccentricities indicated a lack of the qualities of mind which made it possible for him to deal with the intricate political problems which it would be necessary to solve in the restoration of Polish independence and the revival of Polish sovereignty.

When the famous musician came to see me in my office at the Department of State, as he did on many occasions after the United States had entered the war, for the purpose of pleading the

cause of his country and of obtaining consent to
the recruiting of a Polish army in the United
States, I could not avoid the thought that his
emotions were leading him into a path which he
was wholly unsuited to follow. With his long
flaxen hair sprinkled with gray and brushed back
like a mane from his broad white forehead, with
his extremely low collar and dangling black
necktie accentuating the length of his neck, with
his peculiarly narrow eyes and his small mustache and goatee that looked so foreign, he appeared to be a man absorbed in the æsthetic
things of life rather than in practical world
politics. My feeling was that I had to deal with
one given over to extravagant ideals, to the
visions and fantasies of a person controlled by
his emotional impulses rather than by his reason
and the actualities of life. I was impressed by
his fervid patriotism, and by his intense devotion
to the cause of Poland, but it was not unnatural
to think that so temperamental a nature would
be swayed by sentimentality in the advocacy of
a course of action and would give passionate
support to his ideas with little regard to logic
or practical considerations.

Holding this impression of Mr. Paderewski, an

impression which I believe was shared by many of those with whom he came in contact in those early days of his active work for his country, I confess that I was not disposed to give the weight to his opinions that I did later. I liked him personally. I was glad to see him enter my office, for I always found pleasure in talking with him. I admired the intensity of his advocacy of Polish independence and the patriotism which had induced him to abandon his musical career so that he might devote his life to the cause of his country. His cordiality of manner and address was very attractive. He was a likable, I think I may say a lovable man in every sense of the term. Yet at the time of which I am speaking there was the ever-present sense that he lived in the realm of musical harmonies and that he could not come down to material things and grapple with the hard facts of life. It seemed as if he could not realize the difficulties of the part which he had chosen to play in the tragical drama of world affairs. In truth, I thought that he was making a mistake.

This was my early impression of Mr. Paderewski. It was only with time and with a fuller knowledge of the man that I learned how wrong

Paderewski

this impression was and how completely I had
failed to estimate correctly his attainments and
his real mental strength. The new impression,
which I feel is the true one, did not at once sup-
plant the old. It came by degrees and only over-
came the first impression by observation of facts
which could not be successfully questioned or
denied. Possibly it is erroneous to term this
later view an impression, as it is based on
substantial evidence. It may be more exact to
term it a conviction.

That the change was not more immediate and
did not earlier remove my first impression was
due, I think, in no small measure to a mental
attitude common to the majority of men in
judging personality, and that is the attitude
caused by the strength and tenacity of a first
impression even when it has little substance in
fact on which to rest. The psychology of favorable and unfavorable estimates of capacity, and
of the relative value of apparent contradictions
in traits of character, has to do very much with
first impressions and with the receptivity of the
mind of the observer. In studying these I believe that it will be found to be a rule with few
exceptions that first impressions acquired on cas-

ual acquaintance sink deep into the mind and are not easy to change or eradicate.

I found, at least, that this was true in the case of Mr. Paderewski. For a musician of his genius, which necessarily implied a nature sensitive and responsive to emotional influences and to the æsthetic beauties of art, to be transformed, as it were overnight, into a cool, hard-headed statesman dealing wisely with rough and ugly facts, seemed to deny all common experience. It was hard to believe that such a complete change of thought and object in life was real. But, as the Polish hope of independence developed into a certainty, and as Mr. Paderewski became more and more prominent in moulding the policies and directing the activities of the Polish organizations in this and other countries, I was compelled hesitatingly but very gladly to revise my judgment and recognize that my first impression was wrong; I think that I may say that it was unjust, though excusable.

My second impression — and it is the impression that I still hold — was that Ignace Paderewski was a greater statesman than he was a musician, that he was an able and tactful leader of his countrymen and a sagacious dip-

Paderewski

lomat, and that his emotional temperament,
while it intensified his patriotic zeal and his
spirit of self-sacrifice, never controlled or adversely affected the soundness of his judgment or
his practical point of view.

The first direct evidence of his capacity as
a leader which impressed me was his successful
effort to unite the jealous and bickering Polish
factions in the United States and to obtain their
common acceptance of the authority of the
National Polish Council in Paris. Others had
attempted the task and failed. Factionalism had
been the vice and weakness of the old Kingdom
of Poland. With the brightening hope of a Polish
republic this national evil seemed to revive. I
am convinced that Mr. Paderewski was the only
Pole who could have overcome this menace to
the cause of Poland, a menace since it seriously
impaired the possibility of the recognition of
the National Council at Paris by the Allies. His
powers of persuasion, which seemed to spring at
once into being with his entry upon a political
career, his enthusiastic confidence in the resur-
rection of Poland as an independent state, and
his entire freedom from personal ambition made
him the one man about whom the Poles, regard-

Paderewski

less of faction, appeared to be willing to rally. It was a great achievement, a triumph of personality, a tribute to, as well as an evidence of, the faith of a people in the unselfish patriotism of a national leader, which they confirmed later by choosing him to be the premier of the new government. What others, certainly more experienced than he in public affairs and credited with greater political shrewdness, failed to accomplish, Mr. Paderewski accomplished. His success in thus harmonizing the Polish factions gave him at once a preëminence in the councils of his nation which other governments were quick to perceive and to respect.

From the time that Mr. Paderewski assumed a commanding position in the affairs of Poland my early impression of him began to change. I realized that I had failed to appreciate his innate genius for political leadership which proved to be so effective in circumstances that would have tried the sagacity of a man long in public life. Raw amateur though he was in politics—and I mean no disrespect in so characterizing him — nearly everything that he said and nearly everything that he did seemed to be the right thing. He made few mistakes and he never seemed to be in doubt as to the course which he should take. He was wonderfully resourceful and apparently had an instinctive sense of the possible and the practicable. He held his imagination in leash as he did his emotions. He was not carried away with extravagant hopes or unrealizable dreams. His views were essentially sane and logical.

If I had needed further proofs to induce me to revise my impression of the Polish leader who had done so much for his country in connection with the Polish movement in the United States, where his patriotic fervor was a constant inspiration to his countrymen, his subsequent conduct in Warsaw and Paris would have been all-sufficient for that purpose. Without change in the simplicity and frankness of his nature or in his unaffected geniality, he showed a poise of character in dealing with subjects vital to the future of Poland, a conservative judgment, and a calm and unexcitable manner of discussing matters of difference, which gave weight to his words and added greatly to his influence as a negotiator.

The highly developed artistic nature of Mr. Paderewski seemed to be a very weak foundation on which to build the career of a statesman. It appeared incongruous, almost fantastic, to consider it as a possibility. One faced with the amazing fact would, not without reason, declare it to be impossible for a man, whose years up to middle age had been devoted to the developing and perfecting of his ability as a musician, to become without other preparation a public official who could effectively take part in the affairs of state. That was, I know, a common judgment concerning Mr. Paderewski's sudden entrance into public life. It was declared openly and frequently. But the judgment was wrong. He abandoned his music, which had been his very life, and threw himself into the work of politics with the same ardor and devotion that he had shown in following the impulses of his incomparable genius. As thousands had applauded his mastery of harmony, so thousands came to applaud the intensity of his patriotism and the sacrificial spirit with which he laid down his beloved music for the cause of his country.

How fitting it was that Mr. Paderewski should be the one to sign, in behalf of Poland, the treaty that broke the shackles which she had worn so long and which proclaimed to all the world that

Paderewski

Polish independence was an accomplished fact. Imagine, if you can, the thoughts and emotions of the eminent Pole as he advanced to the table in the center of the Hall of Mirrors at Versailles and affixed his signature to the document that bore witness to the triumph of the cause to which he had given his all. The 28th of June, 1919, was a great day to the delegates of the assembled nations, but it was the greatest in the life of Ignace Paderewski.

What Mr. Paderewski has done for Poland will cause eternal gratitude. What he gave up for Poland will cause widespread regret. His response to the cry of his country suffering in the throes of its rebirth is one of the finest examples of true patriotism that an historian has ever had the privilege to chronicle. His career is one which deserves to be remembered not only by his countrymen, for whom he did so much, but by every man, to whom love of country and loyalty to a great cause stand forth as the noblest attributes of human character.

As I review in my mind all the circumstances, I think that it was natural that my first impression of Mr. Paderewski was that which I have attempted to describe and that this impression

faded and disappeared as time and events disclosed, in place of Paderewski the great artist,
Paderewski the great statesman of Poland. It is
this second impression that lives. The first is an
almost forgotten memory. I can to-day think of
Mr. Paderewski only as the zealous advocate of
Polish independence, as the sagacious statesman,
as the tactful negotiator, and as the unselfish
public servant who sought only the welfare of his
country and of its people. It is a fortunate nation,
indeed, which can claim such a man among its
sons, and he is a fortunate man who can leave to
posterity such a memory of generous service.

In giving one's impressions of a personality
such as I have endeavored to portray, it is
difficult not to speak in superlatives. Everything about Mr. Paderewski and his career
invites the superlative form of expression. The
beauty of his character, the fineness of his
sentiments, the loftiness of his ideals, and the
sensitiveness and modesty of his nature, constitute the highest impulses that control human
conduct. A man possessing these qualities —
and Mr. Paderewski has shown that he possesses
them — exercises a deep influence on his fellow-
men, deeper than he himself can ever realize.

Paderewski

Though this recitation of Mr. Paderewski's characteristics may seem to some to give him too fulsome praise and to exaggerate his virtues and attainments, I would not be candidly expressing my views if I said less. His personality through intimate association excited a sympathetic interest which, it is fair to presume, gave color to the impression that it made on my mind. That may be and, I believe, ought to be admitted. But in spite of the favorable interest thus created I do not think that it affected the estimate of Mr. Paderewski's character by unduly magnifying his talents and achievements or by minimizing his faults and failures. An unjustifiable impression, as a rule, grows weaker through continued intercourse with a man and through a fuller knowledge of his intellectuality and his spiritual nature. There was no such experience in the case of the later impression made upon me by this Polish leader. It did not grow weaker; it grew stronger as events justified it and as acquaintance gave me a clearer insight into his motives and aims.

In addition to the attraction of his personality there was an increasing admiration and respect for the man as a leader of public thought and as

Paderewski

a diplomat who would not resort to deceit or intrigue in seeking to obtain his ends, however laudable those ends might be or however strong the temptation to use any means to attain them. Honesty of means as well as honesty of purpose was evident in his conduct as a negotiator. If he misstated a fact, one felt instinctively that it was the result of incomplete knowledge or erroneous information, and was not an intentional suppression or perversion of the truth. Confidence in his integrity was the natural consequence of acquaintance and intercourse with Mr. Paderewski, and it was the universality of this confidence that made him so influential with the delegates to the Peace Conference.

What I have written is the impression which the Prime Minister of the Polish Republic made upon me during our association at Paris and the way that that impression grew and developed in spite of views based on preconceived ideas of his capacity and talents. It has not been as difficult to analyze this change of thought as it has been to account for the radical change in the life and activities of Ignace Jan Paderewski himself. So unnatural a conversion of æsthetic genius into a genius for statecraft without going through a

Paderewski

gradual process of transformation seems to be an anomaly which defies a satisfactory explanation. That it took place is a fact, an extraordinary fact, that must be accepted for the simple reason that it is fact. In history as in memory there will always live two Paderewskis, Paderewski the master of music, and Paderewski the statesman of Poland.

THE END

The Riverside Press
CAMBRIDGE . MASSACHUSETTS
U . S . A